MODERN WORLD NATIONS

Israel

Second Edition

Donald J. Zeigler
Old Dominion University

Series Editor
Charles F. Gritzner
South Dakota State University

CHELSEA HOUSE
PUBLISHERS
An imprint of Infobase Publishing

Frontispiece: Flag of Israel

Cover: The port city of Jaffa, with Tel Aviv in the distance.

Israel, Second Edition

Copyright © 2007 by Infobase Publishing

Chelsea House
An imprint of Infobase Publishing
132 West 31st Street
New York NY 10001

Library of Congress Cataloging-in-Publication Data

Zeigler, Donald J., 1951-
   Israel / Donald J. Zeigler. — 2nd ed.
        p. cm. — (Modern world nations)
   Includes bibliographical references and index.
   ISBN 0-7910-9210-0
1. Israel—Description and travel—Juvenile literature. 2. Israel—History—Juvenile literature. I. Title. II. Series.
   DS117.Z45 2006
   956.94—dc22   2006014242

Series and cover design by Takeshi Takahashi

Printed in the United States of America

Bang Hermitage 10 9 8 7 6 5 4 3 2 1

This book is printed on acid-free paper.

All links and Web addresses were checked and verified to be correct at the time of publication. Because of the dynamic nature of the Web, some addresses and links may have changed since publication and may no longer be valid.

Table of Contents

Israel

Second Edition

CHAPTER 1

Introducing Israel: Ancient Land, Modern Peoples

One region of the world has been known for millennia as the "Holy Land." On the map today, it is called Israel, a country created for the Jewish people after World War II. But another group of people who live there think of it by a different name, Palestine. These people are the Palestinian Arabs, most of whom are Muslims (adherents to the Islamic religion) and a few of whom are Christians. To all three religions—Judaism, Islam, and Christianity—this small region sandwiched between the Mediterranean Sea and the Jordan River has been the scene of some of history's most important religious events. It was traversed by Abraham, seen by Moses, walked by Jesus, and journeyed to by Muhammad—the central figures of the three faiths. Israel is not large in territorial extent, covering an area about the size of New Jersey. But the events that have taken place there, including in the Holy Land's most sacred city, Jerusalem, have led to centuries of competition for its control.

The last decade of the twentieth century in the Holy Land held great promise for a reconciliation between Jews and Palestinians. No sooner had the twenty-first century opened, however, than a new round of uprisings began as Palestinian Arabs renewed their objections to living under the sovereignty of Israel. Both Jews and Palestinians want an independent state of their own. The Jews already have one, the State of Israel; the Palestinians do not. The creation of Israel was meant to give Jews a homeland to which they could return, something they had not had for more than 2,000 years. In creating a Jewish homeland, however, another people lost theirs—the Palestinian Arabs. The Jews of Israel look to the Jews of North America, Europe, and elsewhere for support. The Palestinians look for support to the other Arab peoples of the world, many of whom are powerful because their countries contain vast reserves of oil. For cultural, religious, and economic reasons, conflict in the country now identified as Israel has commanded worldwide attention.

Even at its most basic, the political map of Israel is complex. First, there is the State of Israel, now home to more than one-third of the world's Jews. Second, there are the Palestinian Territories, best known as the West Bank and the Gaza Strip. The West Bank (which was part of Jordan before 1967) continues to be occupied by Israeli security forces; Gaza (which was part of Egypt) saw all Israeli troops withdrawn and all Jewish settlements removed in 2005. In 2006, however, the Israeli Defense Forces re-entered Gaza in response to aggressive actions by the military wing of a Palestinian political party known as Hamas. Third, there are the Golan Heights, a region that was part of Syria prior to 1967, and is now an area disputed between these two nations. The Golan Heights have been annexed to Israel; the Palestinian Territories have not. To these three must be added the metropolitan area of Jerusalem, which spreads across the boundary between the State of Israel and the West Bank. Some self-rule has been given to the Palestinian people of the West Bank and Gaza, but ultimate power rests with Israeli authorities. In reality, the country of Israel encompasses not one, but two peoples: Israeli Jews and Palestinian Arabs. Their worldviews are at odds and their visions of the future could not be more different. Prospects for peace brighten then dim. Not even their powerful allies are able to offer a solution that meets with their approval.

Geographers classify Israel, a country of about 8,000 square miles (20,720 square kilometers), as being very small when compared with other countries in the world. In fact, 46 of the 50 U.S. states are larger than Israel! If Israel were superimposed onto a map of the United States, it would stretch only halfway from San Diego to San Francisco. It is only 250 miles (402 kilometers) from Israel's border with Lebanon in the north to the country's port city of Eilat in the far south. From east to west, it is only 50 miles (85 kilometers) at its widest. Israel's small size and elongated shape figure significantly into its international relations. Together, they invite a feeling of vulnerability. Small states, particularly those with unfriendly neighbors on their borders, sometimes have a hard time surviving. Syria and Lebanon are Israel's two most belligerent neighbors. Egypt signed a peace treaty with Israel in 1979, but only a "cold peace" exists between the two. Jordan signed a peace treaty with Israel in 1994, but the relationship is still troubled. The most significant threat to Israel, however, comes from the Palestinian population within its borders. Egyptian, Jordanian, Syrian, and Lebanese Arabs have independent states of their own. The Palestinian Arabs do not. From their point of view, the land that should be the State of Palestine became, instead, the State of Israel. The Palestinians blame the countries of Europe for not giving them independence immediately after World War I. They also blame the United States for supporting the State of Israel with more foreign aid than it gives to any other country—about $2.5 billion annually in direct payments.

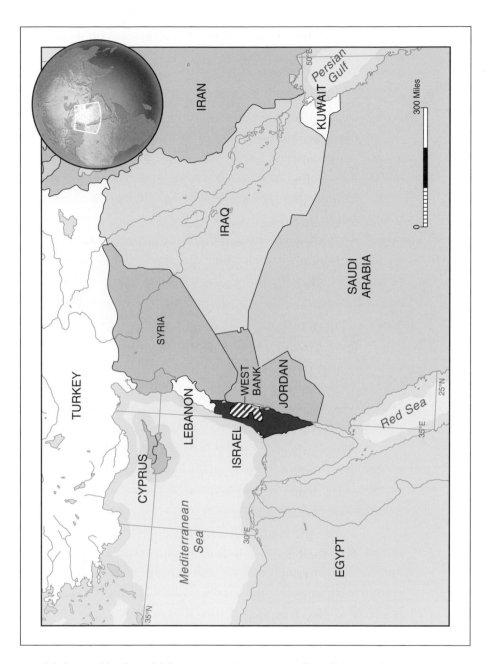

Israel is located in the Middle East, on the eastern edge of the Mediterranean Sea, and shares borders with Egypt, Jordan, Lebanon, and Syria. It is a relatively small country, stretching just 250 miles north to south and 50 miles east to west.

Because Israel was created as a homeland for the Jews, most people think of the population as being rather homogeneously Jewish. In reality, the Jewish population of Israel is extremely diverse. That diversity has been a source of Israel's strength. Jews have returned from around the world—from Europe, Africa, Asia, Australia, and the Americas—to the land of their ancient ancestors. They returned speaking different languages, having different conceptions of Judaism, and being devoted to different ideologies. Some Jews spoke Yiddish (akin to German), some spoke Ladino (a Jewish dialect of Spanish), while others spoke Arabic, Persian, or one of numerous other languages, even English. Jews who came from Europe were mostly secular Jews. They identified strongly as Jews, but were not very religious. In fact, the founding fathers of Zionism (Jewish nationalism) in Europe were largely secular Jews. In the late 1940s, however, very observant Jews began arriving in Israel from Islamic countries in Africa and Asia. They reinvigorated Orthodox Judaism by insisting on observance of their religious laws as set down in their Bible. They joined many "ultra-Orthodox" Jews with roots in Eastern Europe.

Many different ideas about how to run a country also converged in Israel. Some Jews came as socialists because of their European heritage, a few came as capitalists, and the most recent wave of immigrants came as ex-Communists from the former Soviet Union. All of these people joined a small population of Palestinian Jews who had always lived in the Holy Land. Now, the children of these groups go to the same schools, learn the Hebrew language, serve in the same military, and vote in the same elections. Out of such diversity has come vitality, if not unity. There are as many interpretations of Israel's past and as many forecasts of Israel's future as there are Jews. All, however, are thankful to have a "homeland," a state of their own, after more than 2,000 years of living as minority populations in other countries where they often faced discrimination and persecution. That persecution peaked in the twentieth century when Nazi Germany began a campaign, now referred to as the

Holocaust, to exterminate the Jewish people. For anyone who was a Jew, it was a time of terror, torture, and fear. After the 1945 defeat of Germany in World War II, many people saw the creation of a state for the Jews as a necessity for a people who for too long had been the world's "underdogs."

Not only Jews live in Israel, however. There are also Muslims and Christians, most of whom are Palestinian Arabs. A Muslim is someone who submits to the "will of Allah." Allah is the Arabic word for "God." God's word is recorded in the Koran (Qu'ran), their holy book. The religion of Muslims is called Islam, which means "submission." Muhammad is their chief prophet. He was the messenger of God, but not God on Earth. Palestinian Arabs may also be Christians. A Christian is someone who follows the "Word made flesh," that is, the teachings of Jesus of Nazareth, whom they consider to be the Christ, or Messiah, "the promised one," a divine savior sent by God to save human beings from the sins of the world. Judaism, Islam, and Christianity all grew out of the belief that there was only one God, a belief called monotheism. All three religions trace their monotheism to one man, Abraham. In fact, Jews, Christians, and Muslims are all the "children of Abraham." A common ancestry, however, has not prevented them from squabbling with one another over the course of many centuries.

The Palestinians today are an Arab people divided into three groups by geographical boundaries. First, are those who live in the State of Israel as citizens. Second, are those who live in the West Bank and Gaza, some of whom are there as refugees from the rest of Israel. They do not hold Israeli citizenship. Third, are those who live in the surrounding Arab states of Jordan, Syria, and Lebanon. These Palestinians are refugees from the many wars between Israel and the Arab states. Some live in refugee camps, others have taken up residence in the countries' cities. Jordan's population, in fact, is more than half Palestinian. In all three areas, the Palestinian people include both Muslims (the majority) and Christians. They generally see eye-to-eye on the issue of Palestinian statehood. All Palestinians want a state

Within the Muslim quarter of Old City Jerusalem lies a place sacred to Jews and Muslims alike. Known as Temple Mount to Jews and Haram Al-Sharif to Muslims, the site was once the location of the first Jewish temple in Jerusalem and is today home to the Muslim Dome of the Rock and Al Aqsa Mosque (pictured above).

of their own, just as much as the Jews wanted a state of their own in the period leading up to 1948, when Israel gained independence. In the twenty-first century, however, the Palestinians have become the "underdogs," a people without a country of their own, a people oppressed.

Even place names vary between Jews and Palestinians. For the same land, Jews use the name Israel; Palestinians use the name Palestine. Jerusalem is the Jewish name for the holy city. Al Quds, "the holy," is what the Palestinians call it. Within the walled city of Jerusalem, even individual sites have alternative names. Mount Moriah, or the Temple Mount, is what Jews call the ridge on which the ancient Hebrew Temple was located. To the ancient Jews, the Temple was the holiest place in the world. Muslims call the Temple Mount, the same ridge, Haram Al-Sharif, "the holy sanctuary." It is where their Dome of the Rock is located; it is also the site of one of the holiest mosques, called Al Aqsa. By whatever name, the eastern ridge in the Old City of Jerusalem is sacred. Between Jerusalem and the Jordan River is a region called the West Bank by the Palestinians, but the Jews insist on using its Biblical names, Judea and Samaria. Israelis resist using the term *occupied territories* in reference to Judea and Samaria, but Palestinians refer to them as the *illegally occupied territories.* The Sea of Galilee also has competing names, Galilee being the one used by Christians. Jews prefer the Kinneret after the Hebrew word for harp, a reference to its shape; they also call it Lake Tiberias after the largest (and historically Jewish) town on its shores. Overlooking the Sea of Galilee is a tableland on the border with Syria. Jews call it the Golan Heights; Arabs call it the Jaulan Plateau. In the south, Israel's outlet to the Red Sea is via the Gulf of Eilat; Jordan calls the same body of water the Gulf of Aqaba. The place-name map of Israel is saturated with political meaning. Just as wars are fought with guns and tanks, they are also fought with maps and place names. Whoever controls the land has the power to name, or rename, the places that are there.

2

Natural Landscapes

Israel's land and climate, together with its native plant and animal life, have set the stage for the human drama that has unfolded there. From the country's physical geography have been drawn the essentials of life, the natural resources on which people depend for their existence. The variety of terrain in Israel can be grouped into four major landform regions, including the only place on Earth where a person can stand on dry land more than 1,300 feet (396 meters) below sea level! Israel's climate and natural vegetation range from arid (deserts) and semiarid (short grasslands) to subtropical wet-and-dry (Mediterranean scrubland).

Water features range from frontage on two arms of the world ocean (the Mediterranean Sea and the Gulf of Aqaba, a small arm of the Red Sea) to the landlocked and salty Dead Sea. It is also home to one of the world's best-known freshwater bodies, the Sea of Galilee, the Jordan River, and numerous natural springs. Underground, in

Israel can be divided into four landform regions: the coastal plain, which borders the Mediterranean Sea; a series of limestone hills just to the east of the coastal plain; the rift valley, which borders Jordan in the east; and the Golan Heights, in the northeastern part of the country.

some parts of the country, are important aquifers, layers of water-saturated earth. Because much of Israel is part of the world's dryland environment, the most important elements of the country's physical geography are its various water resources. Although water is scarce, Israel has used technology and engineering skills to use water more efficiently and to make water available throughout the entire country.

LANDFORM REGIONS

Israel can be divided into three major north-south trending, landform regions, plus part of the plateau known as the Golan Heights. Along the Mediterranean is a coastal plain, important for its groundwater resources. It is quite narrow in the north and wider in the south. Marking the coastal plain's eastern boundary is a band of limestone hills, some of which reach 3,000 feet (914 meters) in elevation. These are known as the Hills of Galilee in the north, the Samarian and Judean Hills in the center, and the Negev Hills in the south. Negev is a Hebrew word that means "dry." Israel's third, or eastern region, is formed by the valley occupied by the Jordan River, the Sea of Galilee, the Dead Sea, and the Arava depression. It is part of the Great Rift Valley, a trench that extends from Syria in southwestern Asia to Mozambique in southeastern Africa. Much of Israel's part of the Great Rift Valley is below sea level.

An additional physical region, the Golan Heights, towers over the Sea of Galilee and the northern Jordan River. The Golan were taken from neighboring Syria in the Six-Day War of 1967. They are crowned by a line of extinct volcanoes. The upland region receives more rain than the rest of the country and its relatively flat surface allows much of that rain to seep into the soil. Because of their higher elevation, the Golan Heights are also cooler, so moisture does not evaporate as soon as it falls. Golan water reserves nourish the Jordan River and its important tributary, the Yarmouk. Water on the Golan is the envy of not only Israel, but also of Syria and Jordan. Nothing is more precious in a dry country with a growing population than water resources.

All four landform regions are involved in the territorial disputes between Israelis and Arabs. The Palestinian-settled Gaza Strip occupies the southern part of the Mediterranean coastal plain. The hill country and the rift valley are split between Israel and the Palestinian West Bank. The city of Jerusalem sits astride the crest of the Judean Hills. Its west side is in Israel; its east side (including the Old City) was part of the West Bank until annexed by the municipality of Jerusalem. The Golan Heights are disputed between Israel and Syria.

The Jordan River occupies part of Israel's rift valley. It is not a stream-cut valley. Rather, faulting (the downward movement of large blocks of the earth's crust) formed a huge trough. The broad bottom of the Jordan Valley dropped in relation to the highlands on either side. The tiny Jordan River seems almost undeserving of such a broad bottomland. The Jordan begins with snowmelt in the mountains of Lebanon and natural springs in the northern part of Israel. It flows into the Sea of Galilee and on to the Dead Sea. Today, given the demand for water by a growing population, the Jordan is no more than a small creek by the time it gets to the vicinity of Jericho. Nevertheless, because most of the river forms an international boundary between Israel and Jordan, its political significance is immense. It is here that the famous Allenby Bridge forms an important connection between the east and west banks of the Jordan. Allenby was the general who seized Palestine for Britain in World War I. The Arabs, therefore, call the same structure the King Hussein Bridge after Jordan's late monarch. A large new bridge was built in the 1990s and quietly opened in 2001; however, its potential to bridge the gap between Israelis and Arabs is still unrealized. With its opening, there was hope that international cooperation might restore the Jordan so the river would resemble the larger, stronger stream in which the early

Christians were baptized. Large or small, it is still an important resource for attracting Christian tourists. Just south of the Sea of Galilee, a Jewish kibbutz (collective farm), called Yardenit, has developed a short stretch of the river as a Christian baptism site. Congregations come with their pastors for full immersion in its waters, symbolically at least, the same waters in which Jesus was baptized by his cousin John. Many take small vials of the water home with them as cherished mementoes of their experience in the Holy Land.

Parts of the Jordan Rift Valley extending from north of the Sea of Galilee to south of the Dead Sea are below sea level. The Dead Sea, with a salt content of 33 percent (10 times saltier than ocean water), is the world's saltiest body of water. Because of its high salt content, the water is so buoyant that it is difficult to stay balanced while wading close to shore and one can float like a cork on the surface. There are some large resorts on the coastline of the Dead Sea, and its mineral-rich mud has become a valuable product for skin care. In fact, a major cosmetic industry has developed around the Dead Sea salts, which are turned into a variety of creams and lotions. The mud is turned into soap. The chemical industry also draws upon the water's potassium, magnesium, and bromine content. Potash (potassium chloride), which is used in fertilizers, is extracted from the sea's mineralized waters. Bromine is used to make pesticides, fire-retardant plastics, photographic chemicals, and pharmaceutical products. Magnesium is one of the world's lightest metals, just half the weight of aluminum.

Water of the Jordan River has been overutilized, resulting in less of it than ever arriving in the Dead Sea. As a result, the sea is getting smaller and smaller every year, its surface having dropped more than 35 feet (11 meters) since 1960. Much of the sea's water also is lost to evaporation; in fact, the sea has existed in two parts since the 1970s, a larger northern part and a smaller southern part. The Dead Sea and Sea of Galilee present an interesting contrast.

The Dead Sea was so named because it is so salty that no life can exist in its water, not even seaweed. (Recently, however, a microbe was discovered that has adapted itself to such an extreme environment.) The sea is salty because water flows into its basin (via the Jordan River), but there is no stream flowing out of it. Water flowing over land takes on salts. When the water reaches the sea and evaporates, the salts are left behind to accumulate. Along the edge of the Dead Sea, salt pans and salt pillars occur quite frequently. Another unique feature of the sea is that, despite its being the lowest body of water on Earth (now more than 1,300 feet, or 396 meters, below sea level), its low elevation is not what makes the Dead Sea salty. The Sea of Galilee is 700 feet (213 meters) below sea level, but it is a freshwater lake. Streams flow into and out of the Sea of Galilee, keeping the salt content from building up in the water. That is why the Sea of Galilee is the main source for Israel's National Water Carrier, while the water in the Dead Sea is useless. One is filled with fresh water, the other with salt water.

One interesting long-term development plan for the Dead Sea is the construction of a large pipeline or canal that would carry water from the Gulf of Aqaba northward. The difference in elevation between the two bodies of water is about 1,300 feet (396 meters). This would allow water to flow downhill into the Dead Sea under the force of gravity alone. The flow could be harnessed to produce hydroelectric energy that would benefit several countries of the region. Some of that energy could be used to expand water desalination operations. As a bonus, the water itself would replenish the Dead Sea and become part of a restoration effort. It would also help sustain the Israeli and Jordanian chemical industries. Currently, the project has gained the support of both countries, plus the Palestinian Authority. In 2006, a feasibility study was begun to determine the environmental impact of such a large-scale project. From the Dead Sea south, a deep but dry valley, the Arava (Arabah), continues to the Gulf of Aqaba, which

The Dead Sea lies on the border between Israel and the West Bank on the west and Jordan on the east. It is approximately 1,339 feet (408 meters) below sea level–the lowest body of water on Earth. The sea's salt deposits are important to the local economy, and other minerals, such as potash, magnesium, and calcium chloride, are extracted from the sea.

(along with the Red Sea) is but a submarine portion of the same rift.

CLIMATE AND NATURAL VEGETATION

Climate is the long-term average condition of a location's weather. Climate regions are areas of the earth's surface that share common weather patterns. Climate is usually defined on the basis of two major variables, temperature and precipitation. Geographers are particularly interested in the seasonal changes of weather such as hotter and colder, or wetter and drier seasonal patterns. Natural vegetation is closely correlated with climate, although human activities (such as agriculture, urbanization, and fire) have had a major impact on vegetation and its associated animal communities in Israel.

Moisture and Plant Life

Israel is part of the great dry realm that stretches from the shores of the Atlantic Ocean to Southwest Asia and on into Central Asia. Parts of Israel receive less than 10 inches (25 centimeters) of rainfall a year and are classified as arid. The southernmost parts receive less than 1 inch (2.5 centimeters). They are true deserts, areas "deserted" of water and vegetation. At the other extreme are the well-watered hills in the far north. Across the border in Lebanon are even higher mountains, where snow cover builds up during the winter. Some of their meltwaters flow into Israel. Hills and mountains, even in dry climates, are usually able to coax some water out of the atmosphere. As a result, northernmost Israel is naturally forested.

Most of Israel, however, is neither desert nor forest. It is covered by vegetation known as *maquis*, a French word meaning "scrubland." It consists of short trees (such as oaks and carob) and large shrubs, and is the typical vegetation found around the Mediterranean rim except in desert portions of North Africa. (Chaparral is what it would be called in Southern California.) Maquis is vegetation stunted by the frequent wildfires that sweep across the land during the dry summer months. The natural landscape has been further degraded by many centuries of pasturing animals (especially sheep and goats) and growing crops. Without fire, crop agriculture, or grazing, forests of pine, cypress, and eucalyptus (an Australian import) thrive in a Mediterranean climate. What forests remained in Ottoman Palestine in the nineteenth century, however, were cut to fuel the trains that traveled south to Mecca, Arabia, the world's most important pilgrimage city for Muslims. The Ottomans needed wood to keep their steam engines pumping.

In 1948, newly independent Israel inherited a landscape that had been largely denuded of trees almost everywhere except the far north. That is why trees have taken on almost sacred status in Israel. They were a rare, yet beautiful and ecologically useful, commodity. Today, it is considered a show of respect to plant a tree in a person's honor. Although trees have been planted throughout much of the country, they are especially conspicuous along the highway connecting Jerusalem to the coast. The entire landscape has been reforested. Outside of Jerusalem is perhaps the most tangible evidence of the role that trees play in Israeli society. Here is found ample evidence that they have become tools in the nation-building process. Next to Mount Herzel, where so many of Israel's prime ministers are buried, is Yad Vashem, a sprawling memorial to the millions of Jews who lost their lives to the Nazis in World War II. It includes a forest dedicated to "the righteous among the nations," that is, to the Gentiles (non-Jews) who assisted Jews during the Nazis' extermination campaigns. In fact, there is a strong tradition of honoring "righteous Gentiles" throughout Jewish history. Oscar Schindler, whose story was told in the book and film *Schindler's List,* is one of the Gentiles honored at Yad Vashem. More than 20,000 men and women have been so honored for rescuing Jews from annihilation in World War II. Beyond Yad Vashem, thousands more trees have been planted in honor of Jews throughout the world. In fact, it is common for Jewish tourists to plant a tree in Israel. It becomes their contribution to building the nation. Ecologically these trees help to restore the landscape, even if they do not all survive. Their leaves break the force of falling raindrops, their roots help hold the soil in place, their branches shelter birds, and their shade slows down evaporation, giving water a chance to sink into the ground. Trees also moderate temperatures.

Although Israel is part of the "dry world," it is not completely dry. Much of it is fertile because of the presence of water. In fact, Israel occupies the southern end of the western

Fertile Crescent, that arc of good farmland that begins in Mesopotamia (Iraq), sweeps across the base of the Anatolian Plateau (Turkey), and veers southward along the east coast of the Mediterranean Sea. Israel's coastal location in the middle latitudes means that westerly winds move in from the Mediterranean Sea and are forced to rise because of the chain of hills and mountains. As they rise, they cool. As they cool, moisture condenses to form rain or, at higher elevations, snow. This type of falling moisture, induced by air rising up mountain slopes, cooling, and falling as rain or snow, is called orographic precipitation. Because the westerly winds blow for a longer period each year in the north, and because the mountains in the north are higher, northern Israel is the wettest part of the country. Some of that water actually originates in the melting snows of Mount Hermon and the other tall peaks of Lebanon.

Precipitation totals range from 40 inches (102 centimeters) on the border with Lebanon to less than 1 inch (2.5 centimeters) on the Gulf of Aqaba (Gulf of Eilat). Hebron, a West Bank city in the hills south of Jerusalem, marks the southernmost extent of the Fertile Crescent. From Hebron to the Nile River, aridity prevails. The unevenness of precipitation in Israel has presented the country with one of its most daunting problems. It has been solved, at least in part, the same way California solved a comparable problem. The plentiful freshwater resources in the north have been channeled to the south. In California, aqueducts bring water to Los Angeles; in Israel, aqueducts bring water to Tel Aviv and the country's south. The 81-mile long National Water Carrier depends on the Sea of Galilee as its main reservoir. It uses pipelines, aqueducts, open canals, and tunnels to bring fresh water to Israel's semiarid and arid realms. It was completed in 1964.

The National Water Carrier is not the only way in which the Israelis have supplemented their scarce water resources. Creative strategies for finding new water resources and conserving the water they already have are constantly in a state of

The Sea of Galilee, also known as Lake Tiberias, is located in northeastern Israel, near the Syrian border. Because it serves as Israel's main source of freshwater, it has been overused, and in recent years water levels have fallen dramatically. This sign, in Hebrew, says: "Caution! Walking down the steps is dangerous due to the low level of water. Danger of falling."

development. Seeding clouds with silver iodide crystals began in 1976. More recently, the Israelis have begun to recycle household effluent, or sewage, for use as irrigation water in the fields. The southern city of Eilat depends almost totally on desalination, which means removing salts from water. Desalination plants draw upon the brackish (slightly salty) groundwater beneath the surface. Water has even been brought to Israel by ship from Turkey. Of course, there is great emphasis on conservation as well.

Temperature

Israel and Southern California both lie on the western side of a continent and occupy the same belt of latitude. As a result, not only do they share similar precipitation patterns, they also share similar temperatures. Both have a Mediterranean-type climate. It is also called a subtropical wet-and-dry climate. The word *subtropical* reveals something about Israel's relative location; it is just north of the Tropic of Cancer. It also reveals something about temperature patterns; summers are hot and winters are mild. January is Israel's coldest month, but temperatures average about 50° to 54° F (10° to 12° C). August is the warmest month, and average temperatures are about 75° (24° C). Daytime high temperatures, however, can be much higher. Heat builds up quickly during the day. Because there is little moisture in the summer air, surface heat dissipates rapidly into the atmosphere, resulting in cooling beginning as soon as the sun sets. From evening to early morning is the most comfortable time of day. Only along the coast and around the Sea of Galilee does the humidity become oppressive.

By using "wet and dry" to describe Israel's climate, attention is called to the country's precipitation patterns. It is wet in the winter (November to May) when the country comes under the influence of westerly winds blowing in off the Mediterranean Sea. It is dry in the summer when the area comes under the influence of the high-pressure cell that moves northward from the Arabian Desert. High pressure means that air is descending and warming, therefore drying things out, rather than raining. Because of the temperature and precipitation patterns, the natural growing season in Israel, and other Mediterranean climates, is in the winter months.

Although Israel does have a wet winter season, it rarely snows. Jerusalem, for example, receives snowfall on the average only two days a year. Only once, in 1950, was the whole country covered with snow. The southern part of Israel is a parched desert region, the Negev, which is an Asian extension of the great Sahara. The Jordan River valley is also a desert, but of a different kind. It lies in the "rain shadow" of the Judean Hills. As winds pass over the hill country of Israel's central axis, they loose their moisture on the Mediterranean side creating a bountiful ground-water reserve in the hills and under the coastal plain. On their way down the eastern slopes, the leeward side of the Judean Hills, the winds warm up and consequently start absorbing moisture. The Jordan River valley, from the Sea of Galilee all the way to the Gulf of Eilat is a "rain shadow" desert. In fact, standing atop the Mount of Olives in Jerusalem, which is located along the crest of the Judean Hills, provides two different views. Looking west, one sees a typical Mediterranean landscape. Looking east, one sees a desert, a land devoid of all vegetation except along the *wadis,* or intermittent streambeds, that wind out of the hills and into the Jordan Rift Valley below.

SOILS

Soil types in Israel vary with climate and underlying geology. The most common soils are known as *terra rosa,* or "red earth" soils. They develop on limestone terrain under the influence of winter rains and summer droughts. They are red because the iron (red) and aluminum (yellow) components remain behind, while the calcium dissolves and is carried away. It may take 3,000 years to form 1 inch (2.5 centimeters) of topsoil in Israel's Mediterranean climate, which means that soil is a resource to be treasured. Also associated with the limestone geology are numerous caves and caverns. In the deserts, soils are thin and without organic matter. They also tend to be high in salt con-tent, particularly in the Jordan Rift Valley. In the far north (Galilee and the Golan Heights), soils develop on top of a dark igneous rock called basalt. Sandy soils are typical of the coast itself and alluvial soils develop along streams. With water and good management practices, most of these soils have been developed into highly productive agricultural land.

WILDLIFE

Associated with the major ecosystems of Israel are distinct communities of wildlife. Two unique ecosystems, in fact, have become tourist attractions. First, offshore from Eilat are the coral-reef communities and their associated species of anemones, sponges, sea urchins, and tropical fish. These reefs are built by tiny polyps. They live in colonies and extract calcium from the sea water and use it to build their skeletons. When the polyps die, their skeletons remain behind building a coral reef. These colorful underwater features have become important to Eilat's tourism industry. A second type of unique ecosystem comprises the vibrant animal communities that congregate around freshwater springs in the desert. One such spring is known as Ein Gedi; it is along the shore of the Dead Sea. Not only is Ein Gedi lush with vegetation, it is also attractive to animals that come to drink—gazelles, ibex, and panthers—and humans who come there to see the animals. Throughout the country, there are hundreds of species of birds, from coastal gulls to inland quail. There are numerous other members of the animal kingdom, including three species of poisonous snakes (two vipers and a species of cobra) and even black widow spiders. On the coastal plain, even Egyptian mongooses might make an appearance.

Israel and the Palestinian Territories cover only a small area of Earth's surface, but they contain many diverse natural landscapes. As the country's population has increased, changes have come to the natural environment, not all of which are good. Many swamps were drained to create farmland, for instance, something that probably would not be acceptable with today's more enlightened environmental attitudes. Nowhere in the region, however, may water be taken for granted. Nevertheless, it is remarkable how productive the dry lands can be. In so many ways, Israel has, indeed, made the desert bloom.

3

History of Two Peoples

The modern Israelis trace their identity to the ancient Israelites, a people who were forged into a single nation by Moses. According to historical tradition, Moses led them out of captivity in Egypt. He led them to "the Promised Land," then known as Canaan. The modern Palestinians trace their identity to the Arab conquest in the seventh century A.D., but their namesakes appeared on the map as residents of Canaan. They established themselves first along the coast as the Philistines. In fact, since their version of Arabic has no "P" sound, Palestine is correctly pronounced with an initial "F." Both the Israelis as Israelites and the Palestinians as Philistines appeared in history more than 3,000 years ago, as recorded in the Hebrew Bible. The most famous story of the conflict between the two peoples is about David and Goliath. David was an Israelite, and Goliath was a Philistine.

Well before the western Fertile Crescent came to be inhabited by the Philistines and Israelites, however, people of Stone Age and

Bronze Age cultures inhabited the region. In fact, some of the world's earliest settlements were in Israel. The West Bank town of Jericho, for instance, boasts of being the oldest town on Earth with remains dating back to 8000 B.C. The ancient Israelites, under Joshua, had to conquer it before they entered Canaan. The ancient *tel* of Jericho (today the archaeological site called Tel Es-Sultan) is within sight of the modern Palestinian village called Jericho. A tel is an artificial hill, of the type seen throughout the Middle East. Tels are formed by successive cities being demolished and others being built on their remnants. They are treasure troves of artifacts.

From the top of the ancient tel of Jericho, it is easy to understand why a settlement developed there. The climate is hot and dry; it is a rain-shadow desert. But one critical resource is abundantly available at Jericho: water. On one side of the settlement was Elisha's spring and not far beyond was the Jordan River. On the other side of the town was a wadi, a small stream that sprang from the Judean Hills and flowed into the rift valley below. All of this fresh water turned the desert green. Jericho occupies a natural oasis. It is located in an ideal environment for people to farm and for a growing population to begin settling in one place, thereby creating a city. At the same time, Jericho is protected by the desert, which spread beyond the oasis in all directions.

JEWISH IDENTITY

The ancient united kingdom of Israel was created from the 12 tribes of Israelites by the poet-king David. By tradition, it is his star, the six-pointed Star of David, which occupies the center of the modern Israeli flag. On the flag, it is joined by two horizontal bars, reminiscent of a traditional prayer shawl. The Star of David is also known as the Magen David (literally, "shield of David"), yet it is a relatively recent symbol of Israel and the Jewish people worldwide. The Israeli equivalent of the Red Cross is called the Magen David Adom in Hebrew. In Israel, it would not be appropriate to use the name Red Cross, because the cross is a symbol of Christianity.

More than 3,000 years ago, King David conquered a small village in the Judean Hills and made it his capital. He called the city Jerusalem. Since then, it has often been called the City of David. It was there that David's son King Solomon built the First Temple to Yahweh, the God of the Jews. After that, Jerusalem became the center of the Jews' spiritual universe. Jews believed that by being in Jerusalem, as they always were during the high holy days, they were as close to God as they could get. The temple was literally where God resided; it was his house. Israel, as it had been united under kings David and Solomon, lasted for less than a century. Upon Solomon's death, the kingdom split into two parts: Israel in the north and Judah in the south. Conquest followed.

The prosperous northern kingdom, known as "Israel," was conquered by the Assyrian Empire in the eighth century B.C. The less prosperous southern kingdom, known as "Judah," was conquered by the Babylonian Empire in the sixth century B.C., and the First Temple was destroyed. In both cases, the Jews were taken to Mesopotamia and prohibited from living in their ancient holy land. When the Babylonian Empire was conquered by the Persians, however, exiles from Judah were permitted to return to Jerusalem, and some did. The Second Temple was built upon their return. That temple was the one rebuilt by King Herod, one of the great "builder kings" of history, just before the birth of Jesus. Herod's temple was destroyed by the Roman Empire in A.D. 70. It has never been rebuilt, in Jerusalem or anywhere else. Between 63 B.C., with the Roman siege of Jerusalem, and A.D. 1922, the following empires have ruled the Holy Land: Roman Empire, Byzantine Empire, several Muslim empires, a Crusader Kingdom, and the Ottoman Empire. For 2,000 years, most of the world's Jews lived in countries other than their own.

The Diaspora—the flight of Jews from their ancestral homeland—began in A.D. 70. It almost seemed to be a repeat of their exile in Babylon centuries earlier. For nearly two millennia, Jews lived in many places throughout the world, but not in their ancestral homeland. By the late nineteenth century, only 25,000 Jews lived in Palestine. They were concentrated in Jerusalem, Tiberias (on the Sea of Galilee), and Safed (in Galilee), where they lived under Ottoman rule. Most of the world's Jews lived scattered across the Mediterranean basin, Europe, Asia, and, later, in the Americas and Australia. Some lived as far away as India and China. Wherever these Diaspora Jews lived, they were minorities and usually were treated as such. Most lived in rural villages or urban ghettos. Ghetto, in fact, is an Italian word meaning foundry. It comes from Venice, where the site of a former foundry was walled off to become the Jewish quarter of the city. It was where Jews were forced to live beginning in 1516. After that, ghetto came to refer to any urban neighborhood where Jews lived. Only recently has it been used as a synonym for any part of a city where members of a minority group live because of economic, social, or legal forces.

Archaeology is a national sport in Israel, and archaeologists—Yigael Yadin, for instance—are as well known as athletes. One of the driving forces in the creation of the State of Israel was the belief that the destiny of the Jewish people was to occupy the Holy Land. As a result, upon returning to the eastern Mediterranean from the Diaspora, they began to look for links between their ancient and modern history. Archaeology filled a national need, and a few sites emerged as symbols of the nation-building process. The most dramatic one is Masada. It is a large, isolated mesa that overlooks the Dead Sea. On its flat top, deserted of all vegetation, there once existed a settlement of Jews. The settlement began as a fort, but was turned into a getaway palace by King Herod the Great. After Herod, Masada was used as a refuge by Jews fleeing Jerusalem as the city was being destroyed by the Roman legions. These refugees, numbering about a thousand, were known as Zealots because of the zeal with which they resisted the Roman forces.

Masada, located on an isolated rock plateau above the Dead Sea, is Israel's most famous archaeological site. Named a World Heritage Site by UNESCO in 2001, it once was home to the palace complex of Herod the Great, King of Judea.

On top of Masada, the Zealots tried to defend themselves against the Roman soldiers who were encamped below. They were determined to remain free and dreamed of a future in which they would once again govern themselves as an independent people, as they did under King David. The Romans laid siege to Masada in A.D. 73. First, they cut off supply lines and then they started building earthen ramps to the top of the mesa. The Zealots did not surrender, though. Rather, they decided on a course of action that was made clear to the Romans when they broke through the defensive wall on top of the mount. All the Romans encountered was silence. The Zealots had committed suicide rather than submit to the authority of Rome. They drew lots to see who would go first. The determination of the Zealots to live free has been turned into the determination of the modern Israelis to make monumental sacrifices to remain in their Holy Land. The archaeological work of Yigael Yadin lends little credence to the mass-suicide story. But Israeli Jews like to believe in the tale as told by Eleazar Ben Yair, leader of the Zealots, as recorded by the historian Flavius Josephus in *Jewish Wars*, which was written from secondary sources less than a decade after it happened:

> My loyal followers, long ago we resolved to serve neither the Romans nor anyone else but only God . . . ; now the time has come that bids us prove our determination by our deeds. . . . it is evident that daybreak will end our resistance, but we are free to choose an honorable death with our loved ones. . . . Let our wives die unabused, our children without knowledge of slavery. . . . Let us die unenslaved by our enemies, and leave this world in company with our wives and children.

Clearly, there was a siege, and at least some of the Jews on top of Masada probably resisted conquest to their last breath. What is important today to the Jewish people, however, are not the facts of history. Rather, it is the important role that Masada has played in building a national identity.

PALESTINIAN IDENTITY

Just as the Jews found events in their history around which to forge an identity, so, too, have the Palestinians. Two events stand out. One was the Arab conquest of the Fertile Crescent. The other was the Arab Revolt of 1916–1917. It is important to note that Palestinian history is Arab history. Palestinians identify themselves first and foremost as being an Arab people. The name "Palestinian" indicates that these particular Arabs are from the land called Palestine. Their cousins are the Syrian and Egyptian Arabs, among others. In fact, the Arab World stretches from Morocco to Iraq and Yemen.

Within a few years of the Prophet Muhammad's death in A.D. 632, the Arabs of eastern Arabia who lived around Mecca and Medina came bursting onto the world stage. Taking advantage of a declining Byzantine Empire to the north, they quickly conquered Damascus in Syria and then Jerusalem. By A.D. 642, Palestine was firmly under the control of a new Muslim regime. It was first ruled from Damascus as the Umayyad Empire, then from Baghdad as the Abbasid Empire, and then from Cairo as the Fatimid Empire. All represented a humane, enlightened, and workable relationship between Islamic religious authorities and secular governance. These were the golden years of Arab civilization, when their literature, science, mathematics, and art were the envy of the world. By comparison, in Europe, these were the years of the Dark Ages. Images of the Middle East under Umayyad, Abbasid, and Fatimid rule loom large in the Arabs' collective memory and, by extension, the Palestinian consciousness. They are a reminder of how good life was when they were ruling themselves.

Muslim rule was interrupted by the Crusaders who arrived from western Europe in A.D. 1100 and established Christian kingdoms along the eastern Mediterranean coast. The Crusader Kingdoms lasted for almost two centuries. Their defeat was initiated by the Muslim ruler Saladin. His victory in 1187 at the Battle of Hattin in Galilee marked the beginning of the end of Christian rule in the Holy Land. Shortly after the fall of the last Christian stronghold, Acre (Akko), Muslim rule returned with the conquering Mamlukes, whose power base was in Egypt. Although Crusader and Mamluke rule were far from enlightened, they both left the Holy Land with a layer of new architectural masterpieces. To this day, Jerusalem has some of the finest Crusader and Mamluke architecture in the world.

Mamlukes were replaced by Ottoman Turks as rulers of the Arab lands of the western Fertile Crescent. Beginning in 1516, Ottoman rule lasted more than five centuries. The

Ottomans may have been Muslims, but their rule over the Arabs was not welcome. It was the overthrow of Ottoman rule that provided the other defining moment in Palestinian identity. For Arabs, the first glimmer of hope came when the Ottoman Empire, seated in Istanbul, allied itself with Germany during World War I.

Although they were Ottoman subjects, the Arabs allied themselves with Great Britain, which was fighting to defeat Germany. The British used the Arabs to stage a revolt against the Ottomans in 1916–1917. This became know as the Arab Revolt. It was led by a direct descendent of the prophet Muhammad, Sharif Hussein of Mecca. As the revolt moved northward into Syria and Palestine, Ottoman rule came to an end. By the end of World War I, the Ottoman Empire was all but dismantled, and the Arabs thought they would be rewarded with independent states of their own for helping the British. They were wrong. Palestine and Transjordan (today Jordan) became British mandates. A mandate is like a temporary colony. The League of Nations gave Great Britain the task of taking care of the Arabs until they were ready for independence. To the Arabs, this was interpreted as a betrayal and an insult. Nevertheless, the mandates of Palestine and Transjordan lasted for two decades. Transjordan was eventually granted independence under an Arab king. Palestine was not. It became a homeland for the world's Jews.

By the end of World War I, the Palestinians already knew that the steady stream of Jews disembarking at the port in Jaffa threatened their ability to ever have a state of their own. Their hopes had been so high in 1917, but they faded in the 1920s, and were dashed in 1948, when the State of Israel was created. Still, the promise of the Arab Revolt gave Palestinians a new identity and renewed pan-Arab pride. Like most other Arab states, the Palestinians adopted a version of the flag of the Arab Revolt as their own. It has yet to fly over an independent state of Palestine.

ISRAELI INDEPENDENCE

The modern Israeli state did not come into being until 1948. For the Jews, the creation of Israel was like restoring the Kingdom of David, a kingdom that had not existed for nearly 3,000 years. For the Arabs, the creation of Israel was at their expense; it was an event that became possible only because they were so weak at the time. Until the birth of Zionism in the 1890s, most Jews held to the belief that their return to Jerusalem, also known as Zion, would take place only with the coming of the Messiah. In other words, God would decide when the Jews returned to Zion. The Zionist movement, however, changed all that. Zionism was born in the minds of Diaspora Jews in Europe, one of whom was named Theodor Herzl, a Hungarian-born man living in Austria. He planted the idea of an independent state for the Jews in the thoughts of his people. Herzl lived at a time when the boundaries of Europe were being reshaped by nationalism. It seemed as if every culturally distinct people on the continent had the ambition to have a state of their own. Why shouldn't the Jews?

In 1897, Herzl and other Zionists convened the first World Zionist Congress in Basel, Switzerland. There, they proclaimed to the world that they had lived as persecuted minorities for too long. They recalled a history of being forced to live in ghettos and of being terrorized by pogroms, which were organized massacres of Jews. They wanted a state of their own—a place that every Jew in the world could call home, a place that would assure their survival. Jewish nationalism became known as Zionism.

The events of the twentieth century, especially the Holocaust, only proved their point. The Holocaust was an extermination campaign organized by Adolf Hitler and his Nazi Party. It resulted in the death of six million Jewish men, women, and children, many of whom were killed in gas chambers and burned in ovens. The widespread death camps had names like Dachau, Auschwitz, and Treblinka. After World War II, most of the world agreed that the Jewish people had suffered enough and that they needed a homeland, a state of their own. The Jews wanted their Holy Land, governed since 1922 by the British as the Mandate of Palestine. Resettlement had already begun, first under the Ottomans and then under the British. Jews from Europe, under Moses Montefiore, had purchased land on the outskirts of Jerusalem in the mid-1800s. A settlement was built there overlooking the Old City. But most of the settlement that was to lead to the creation of Israel took place along the coast, north of the city of Jaffa, where sandy and poorly drained (and therefore inexpensive) land was available. These "suburbs" of Jaffa became the city of Tel Aviv, which means "hill [tel] of spring [aviv]." It was a name with a past and a future. More than 2,500 years earlier, during the "Babylonian Captivity," exiles from Judea lived in a place called Tel Aviv in Mesopotamia. The reference to spring in the place name reminded the early Jewish settlers of the sand dunes north of Jaffa that a rebirth lay ahead of them.

True to the demands of Jewish culture, the first public building in Tel Aviv was a school. It was named the Gymnasya Herzeliya after Theodor Herzl. In the first two decades of the twentieth century, Tel Aviv grew into the largest city in Palestine, quickly surpassing Jerusalem. It became the core of the modern Israeli state. Jaffa, called Yaffo by the Jews, became but one of its many, and most picturesque, neighborhoods. Today, Tel Aviv anchors a coastal metropolis of 2.7 million people, which is home to about two out of every five Israelis.

Since independence, the Israelis have fought five wars with their Arab neighbors. The first war was fought in 1948–1949 with the Arabs. It began the day after Israel declared its independence. The second war was fought with Egypt over the Sinai Peninsula and Suez Canal in 1956. The third was the Six-Day War, fought in 1967 against Egypt, Jordan, and Syria. The fourth conflict was the 1973 Yom Kippur War, fought against Egypt and Syria. Finally, in 1982, a war was fought with the

Since the late 1980s, there have been two intifadahs, or Palestinian uprisings, against Israeli military rule, within the country. Pictured here are Palestinian protestors in Gaza City, shortly after the second intifadah began in September 2000.

Palestine Liberation Organization (PLO) in Lebanon. Each war resulted in Israeli territorial gains. In fact, there was some question in 1956 about whether the Israelis would drive all the way to Cairo, Egypt's capital, and in 1973 about whether they would drive all the way to Damascus, Syria's capital. They did not. In fact, much of the territory gained was eventually given back to the country from which it was seized.

In addition to these five wars, there have been two *intifadahs*, or Palestinian uprisings, within Israel. The Arabic word intifadah literally means "shaking off." The first intifadah raged between 1987 and 1993 and then went into an on-and-off lull for the rest of the decade. The second intifadah began in 2000, with the failure of peace talks in the United States. It is often called the Al Aqsa Intifadah, because it began when Ariel Sharon (who was to become prime minister in 2001) ventured onto the Temple Mount where the Al Aqsa mosque is located and which is under the jurisdiction of Palestinian authorities. He was accompanied by a thousand bodyguards. Soon after Sharon's visit, riots broke out in Jerusalem and then in the rest of Israel. Israel responded with military force; the Palestinians responded with terrorism against Israelis. The suicide bomber became the symbol of the second intifadah. A truce was declared in 2005, but by that time the uprising had claimed the lives of a thousand Israelis, mostly civilians, and more than 3,000 Palestinians.

4

People and Culture

The population of Israel, including the Palestinian Territories, is more than 10 million, roughly the same as the state of Michigan. Rarely, however, is the population of the entire country reported. Instead, Israel and the Palestinian Territories are reported separately. The State of Israel itself is home to 6.3 million people, but this figure includes about 187,000 who live in the West Bank and 20,000 who live in the Golan Heights. These Jews inhabit far more than 100 heavily fortified settlements built to solidify Israel's hold on the land beginning in 1967. The population of Israel also includes 177,000 Jewish citizens who now reside in the Old City and in the settlements now annexed to the municipality of Jerusalem. These, too, were built after 1967. In the Gaza Strip, there had been 21 Jewish settlements that housed about 5,000 people. During the summer of 2005, the government of Israel evacuated them all within one week. Now, not a single Jew lives in the Gaza Strip. Its population is entirely Palestinian.

The Palestinian population of the West Bank is 2.4 million (confined to an area of only 2,262 square miles, or 5,860 square kilometers); the population of Gaza is 1.4 million (living in an area of 140 square miles, or 360 square kilometers). Together, the Palestinian Territories have a population density of about 1,600 people per square mile, much higher than the most densely populated U.S. state, New Jersey. The Palestinian population of the territories includes hundreds of thousands of refugees. They were evicted from their homes in towns such as Jaffa, Lydda, and Ein Karem during the Arab-Israeli War of 1948–1949. Additional Palestinian refugees live in Jordan, Syria, Lebanon, and other Arab states. The United Nations has registered a total of 3.6 million Palestinian refugees in the Palestinian Territories and surrounding countries. The Palestinians of the West Bank and Gaza do not hold Israeli citizenship and have no right of free access to the State of Israel. Their citizenship is assigned to the Palestinian Authority, but the government of Palestine is under the sovereignty of Israel. These Palestinians are a people without a state. The territories have not been annexed by Israel, nor have they been given independence. The autonomous, or self-governing, status that had been granted to 40 percent of the West Bank and its Palestinian population diminished during the Al Aqsa Intifadah, but now appears to be more secure.

The State of Israel annexed the Golan Heights in 1981. They were inhabited by Syrian Arabs (who fled in 1967), not Palestinians. The annexation of the West Bank (except for East Jerusalem) and Gaza, however, has never been supported by the Israeli government. The reason for this is clear: Such an action would contradict Israel's status as a Jewish state. If Israel were to annex all Palestinian Territories today, there would be about as many Palestinians in the total population as there are Jews. In a short time, the Palestinian population would be a majority, because the rate of natural increase among the Palestinians is 3.6 percent annually while the rate of increase for Jews is 1.3

percent. At these rates of growth (without any immigration), the population of Jews will double in about 50 years, but the population of Palestinians will double in only about 20 years.

Palestinians have large families, and Israelis, except for the ultra-Orthodox, do not. As a result, Israel must continually face a demographic future in which the Palestinian population becomes ever bigger, while the Jewish population grows only slowly. The gap between the two populations would be even larger were it not for the one million Soviet Jews who have arrived in Israel as immigrants since 1987. There are, however, no other comparably large immigrant streams on the horizon. Today, the only large reservoir of potential Jewish migrants to Israel is the United States, which has a Jewish population larger than Israel's. It is doubtful, however, that millions of American Jews would decide to make *aliyah*, a term meaning "going up" but which is used as the Hebrew word for Jewish immigration to Israel.

GEOGRAPHIC DISTRIBUTION OF THE POPULATION

More than 90 percent of Israel's population lives in urban places of 2,000 or more inhabitants. The three largest metropolitan areas are Tel Aviv, Jerusalem, and Haifa. In fact, Israel seems to be growing its own megalopolis, or giant city, stretching from Haifa along the coast to south of Tel Aviv and then "up" to Jerusalem. The Galilee in northern Israel is also thickly settled, but it is dominated by villages and towns rather than large cities. It is in the Galilee and the coastal city of Akko that most of Israel's Arab citizens outside the Jerusalem metropolitan area live. The southern part of Israel, the Negev Desert, is sparsely populated. Even the Bedouin Arabs, traditional nomads of the Negev and the Judean deserts, are settling down. Government policies, in fact, favor permanent dwellings for the Bedouin. There are currently about 180,000 Bedouin in Israel. Most have roots in the Arabian Peninsula, but those in the north hail from Syria. All are Muslims.

In the West Bank and Gaza Strip, there are three distinct settlement forms. First, there are the Palestinian villages, towns, and cities. The largest are Hebron, Ramallah, Nablus, and Jenin, all in the West Bank. Some smaller settlements are also well known: Bethlehem, a long walk south from Jerusalem, and Jericho, an even longer walk from Jerusalem down into the Jordan Valley. Second, there are the Palestinian refugee camps, most of which have been in existence for more than half a century. Tents have been replaced by cement-block buildings, but their inhabitants still think of their home as being somewhere in Israel itself. Third, there are the Israeli settlements, all of which have been built since the Palestinian Territories were captured in the 1967 war. The refugee camps and the Israeli settlements are stumbling blocks on the road to peace in the Middle East. The start of a resolution, however, was made in 2005 when Israel withdrew all settlers from the Gaza Strip and began to evict settlers from illegal Jewish settlements in the West Bank.

RELIGIOUS DIVERSITY

Even though the State of Israel is thought of as a Jewish state, the 1948 Declaration of Independence ensures "complete equality of social and political rights to all its inhabitants irrespective of religion." In fact, Israel is a land of tremendous cultural diversity. One aspect of that diversity shows up in the religious realm. Four out of every five Israeli citizens are Jews, but one in five is Muslim, Christian, or Druze. Most of these non-Jewish citizens of Israel are Arabs, specifically Palestinian Arabs. These Israeli Arabs (or Arab Israelis) are likely to refer to themselves as "Palestinians with Israeli citizenship." They can vote in national elections, run for office, hold seats in the Knesset (the Israeli national parliament), and attend Israeli universities. Still, unlike Jews, they are not obligated to serve in the military, which is known as the Israeli Defense Force, and few choose to join. In addition, Israeli Arabs may not freely buy land in most areas of Israel. In some respects, they must feel as

The Armenian Orthodox Church has had a presence in Jerusalem since the third century. Here, a group of Armenian Orthodox priests and their archbishop celebrate Ascension Day in the Mosque of the Ascension on Jerusalem's Mount of Olives.

alienated in a Jewish state as did Jews living in various Arab states before moving to Israel.

The Arab population of Israel is religiously diverse. Most Arabs are Muslims, but some (about 1 in 10) are Christians. In fact, Arab Christians are descendants of some of the earliest followers of Jesus. They are divided among a number of churches, the most important of which are the Greek Orthodox, Greek Catholic, and Roman Catholic. In addition, however, there are some thriving Christian populations in Israel that are not Arab. The best known are the Armenians, most of whom belong to the Armenian Orthodox (or Apostolic) Church. In addition, many Western churches believe that it is important to have a presence in the land where Jesus carried on his earthly ministry. They consequently maintain missions and religious orders there even in the absence of many parishioners. For some, serving international Christian pilgrims is their main objective. Even the Church of Jesus Christ of Latter Day Saints (the Mormon Church) maintains a beautiful university in East Jerusalem. Overt evangelism by any Christian group, however, is forbidden in Israel. The diversity of Christianity in Israel, and the relatively small numbers involved, is seen in the following table.

CHRISTIANS IN ISRAEL (2005 estimates)	
Greek Orthodox	46,600
Greek Catholic	45,000
Roman Catholic (Arab)	26,000
Roman Catholic (Other)	25,000
Maronite Catholic Christians	5,500
Judeo-Christians (Messianic Jews)	4,000
Lutherans and Anglicans	3,700
Syrian Orthodox	2,000
Armenian Orthodox	700
Coptic Orthodox	680
Armenian Catholic	400
Syrian Catholic	300
Coptic Catholic	60
Chaldean Catholic	25

The three great monotheistic religions of the Western world are represented in Israel and the Palestinian Territories. Judaism, Christianity, and Islam all trace their heritage back to a single event, the covenant between God and Abraham, whose name means "father of many." What made Abraham's message unique 5,000 years ago was his acceptance of monotheism, the doctrine that there was but one God. It contrasted quite distinctly with the polytheistic beliefs that prevailed at the time. Polytheism is the belief in many gods, primarily the gods of nature. Abraham's beliefs emphasized the unity and brotherhood of all people who would make one commitment: a declaration of loyalty to the one true God and a rejection of idols and idol worship. Abraham and Sarah (along with Isaac, Rebecca, Jacob, and Leah) lie buried in the Cave of Machpelah, located in Hebron (Arabic, "Al Khalil") in the West Bank. Before David moved the capital of a unified Israel to Jerusalem, he ruled from Hebron.

Abraham, the father of many, however, was the father of none until very late in life. He and his wife, Sarah, thought they would always be childless. That is why Abraham took a second partner, Hagar. Ishmael was born to Abraham and Hagar. Muslims trace their descent through Ishmael. Then, Sarah became pregnant and Isaac was born. Jews and Christians trace their descent through Isaac. Jews, Muslims, and Christians around the world consider themselves "the children of Abraham." All three faiths believe in the same God. In Arabic, his name happens to be Allah.

JUDAISM

Jews, Christians, and Muslims are the descendants of Abraham, but each religion has aligned itself with a different major prophet. Abraham may be honored by Jews as their patriarch, but their chief prophet is Moses, the probable author of the first five books of the Hebrew Bible, known as the Pentateuch to Jews. It was Moses who led the ancient Israelites out of captivity in Egypt and forged them into a single nation. Moses was the person to whom God revealed the *decalogue*, what Christians know as the Ten Commandments. Moses said: "If the people of Israel are the people of God, then they must live by God's law; if the people of Israel live by God's law, then they will always be the people of God." The Jews see themselves as "God's chosen people." Many believe that the land of Canaan (Palestine) was promised to them by God.

Jews believe God is merciful, compassionate, and gracious; that he is just, forgives wickedness, and punishes the guilty; and that he is slow to anger and abounding in love. Jews look forward to the messianic age when humanity will enjoy a reign of righteousness and peace, united in the worship of the one God. God's expectations are set out in the Hebrew Bible, which has been supplemented by the Talmud. Together, these writings comprise the *Torah*, or law, in its broadest sense. Judaism places a strong emphasis on these texts and their interpretation. The result has been the evolution of a highly literate culture in which education is central to life and living.

A Jewish house of worship is called a synagogue, which means "meeting place." In North America, temple is also used to designate the place where Jews come together to pray. The original Temple, and the only place where Jews could pray in Solomon's time, stood in Jerusalem. The focal point of the worship service is the chanting of Torah portions by the cantor. He reads from the Torah scrolls. The person who leads the service is the rabbi, a word that means "teacher." The Jewish sabbath is known as Shabbot. It begins at sundown on Friday and ends at sundown on Saturday. It is observed as a day of rest and prayerful reflection. In fact, strict observance of Shabbot means that even such simple tasks as pushing an elevator button are forbidden. Elevators in some hotels, therefore, are programmed to run continuously on Shabbot and to stop on each floor automatically.

In Israel, the Jewish holidays are strictly observed: Rosh Hashanah (New Year) and Yom Kippur (Day of Atonement) begin and end, respectively, 10 days of atonement in September or October. Pesach, known as Passover in the West, anchors the spring; it commemorates the deliverance of the ancient Hebrews

Within Judaism, there are three divisions: Orthodox, Conservative, and Reform. Orthodox Jews adhere to the strictest interpretation and application of the laws first espoused in the Talmud, the authoritative body of Jewish tradition. Here, cohanim, or Jewish Orthodox priests, participate in a blessing during the Jewish holiday of Sukkoth.

from Egyptian bondage. Other holidays—Sukkoth, Shavuot, and Hanukkah—are also important days of celebration. Hanukkah is especially well known in the United States, because it coincides with the Christmas season. The word literally means "festival of lights," so the lighting of candles has become central to its celebration. On each night of Hanukkah, eight days in a row, a new candle is lit on the Hanukkah menorah. The menorah (Hebrew, "candlestick") that has become a symbol of the State of Israel, appearing in its coat of arms, is different from the Hanukkah menorah. The former has only seven arms.

World Judaism is divided into three branches: Orthodox, Conservative, and Reform. In Israel, however, virtually every synagogue is Orthodox. Still, Judaism in Israel is not monolithic.

Jews differ with one another about how to apply the principles of the holy scriptures to life and to the management of the modern state. Some questions have metaphysical dimensions, such as whether the ancient Temple should be rebuilt. Others seem mundane, such as whether buses should run, drivers drive, or stores be open on Shabbot. At one end of the religious spectrum are the Ultra-Orthodox Jews who maintain the customs, including the dress, of eighteenth-century Europe. At the other end are the secular Jews, who live modern lives with little reference to Torah except on the high holy days. In fact, it is not necessary to be religious to be a Jew. The only thing required is to be born of a Jewish mother (or be converted, although this is not actively encouraged). That means another fault line has opened up in Israeli society: the division between religious Jews and secular Jews played out geographically as the division between more traditional Jerusalem and more contemporary Tel Aviv.

ISLAM

Islam (specifically, Sunni Islam) is the majority religion in the Palestinian Territories. It is also an important minority religion in the State of Israel, where about 15 percent of the population is Muslim. Islam originated on the Arabian Peninsula with "The Prophet," a merchant trader named Muhammad. According to Muslim tradition, it was through Muhammad that God revealed an additional, and a final, set of guidelines for how people should live on Earth. In A.D. 610, Muhammad went into his first trance and began to recite. His recitations were later compiled into the Koran (Quran). Muslims believe that the Koran is the direct word of God as revealed to the prophet Muhammad. The Prophet is not divine, but the Koran is. It supersedes all previous scriptures, but the prophets of Judaism and Christianity are respected, as affirmed in this passage from the Koran:

It is He Who sent down to thee (step by step), in truth, the Book, confirming what went before it; and He sent down the Law (of Moses) and the Gospel (of Jesus) before this, as a guide to mankind, and He sent down the criterion (of judgment between right and wrong).

The basic principles that unite followers of the Islamic faith are summed up in the Five Pillars of Islam. Muslims must (1) believe in the one God ("Allah") and in the prophecy of Muhammad; (2) pray five times a day and in the mosque on Friday; (3) keep the fast of Ramadan, a month during which it is forbidden to eat or drink during daylight hours; (4) give alms, amounting to 2.5 percent of savings, to the poor and needy; and (5) if able, make the pilgrimage to Mecca (Muhammad's birthplace) at least once.

Whereas Judaism is a religion for the Jewish people only, Islam is a universal religion. The Koran was given to the Arab people, but the message was meant for all human beings. Muslims, therefore, seek converts. A mosque, or *masjid*, is a Muslim prayer hall. Traditionally, everyone needed to be within "calling distance" of a mosque, so they could get there quickly when it came time to pray. That is why most mosques today have towers attached. Those towers are called *minarets*, and it was from their tops that the *muezzin* would call people to prayers five times a day. The minarets of mosques punctuate the skylines of Islamic cities and towns in Israel and the Palestinian Territories. The taller minarets usually arise from so-called Friday mosques. Today, the calls are issued via loudspeakers. Friday is the holy day for Muslims, and they are obligated to report to a mosque for community prayers around noon. During the prayer service, they also hear a message from the *imam*, the leader of the service. Holy feasts, known as *eids*, punctuate the Muslim year. The two most important are the Eid Al-Fitr, which ends the fast of Ramadan, and the Eid Al-Adha, which commemorates Abraham's willingness to sacrifice Ishmael. Because the Islamic calendar is based on lunar months, these holy days may occur in any season.

DRUZE

The Druze are followers of another important minority religion in Israel. They live primarily in the Galilee, close to Lebanon, the country where most of the world's Druze live. Their religion began as an offshoot of Islam in tenth-century Egypt, but it evolved into a faith that combines Islamic, Judeo-Christian, and other philosophical elements. Muslims no longer consider the Druze to be part of their faith community. Druze think of themselves as being more strict monotheists than Muslims. In fact, they call themselves the Muwahedun (from the Arabic word *wahed*, which means one). They set themselves off from the other monotheistic faiths by honoring Jethro, Moses' father-in law, as their major prophet, by worshipping on Thursday evenings, and by believing in reincarnation.

It is not easy for minority religions to survive in the world. The Druze have done it by using three strategies. First, they became masters of the mountains. They chose as their home the tallest mountains in the eastern Mediterranean, the mountains of Lebanon that stretch into the nearby Galilee. They used their terrain as a fortress, as protection. The mountainous environment also provided them with plentiful rainfall on which they could thrive. Second, they insist that marriages be limited to the Druze community. One Druze marries another Druze, not a Muslim, Christian, or Jew. Third, they turned their religion into a secret creed. In fact, only a small fraction of the Druze, those who elect to become "religious Druze," read and understand their scriptures. Because outsiders have no access to their holy texts, their theology is above criticism. Like Jews, the Druze adhere to an ethnic religion that does not seek converts.

Over many centuries, the Druze living in Israel have become a tightly knit community. Most of them live in less than two dozen villages in the Galilee (with names like Yirka and Hurfaysh), near Haifa, and on the Golan Plateau. They are a proud people who contribute substantially to the well-being of Israel.

Because of their loyalty, Druze serve in the Israeli Defense Force, often holding high-ranking positions.

The best-known group of Druze lives in the Golan, in the territory that was taken from Syria by Israel in 1967. They, too, are loyal, but to Syria. These Druze, concentrated in five villages, have refused Israeli citizenship and fully expect that one day their land, the Golan Heights, will return to Syrian sovereignty. They are rewarded by the Syrians with certain privileges: Their sons and daughters are the only ones permitted to cross the demilitarized zone on the Golan as they go back and forth several times a year to attend Damascus University. There are more than 17,000 Druze on the Golan, which they share with an equal number of Jewish settlers. The Arab population of the Golan left in 1967 and today lives in Syria.

THE BAHA'IS

Jerusalem may be central to Jews, Christians, and Arabs, but the city of Haifa is central to members of the world's Baha'i faith. The elegant headquarters and chief shrine of the Baha'is perch on the slopes of Mount Carmel, and their gardens tumble down to the sea. Why Haifa? Because Bahá'u'lláh, the founder, indicated that this area of northern Palestine should become the faith's permanent home. He, himself, is buried in Akko; his son and chosen successor, Abdul Baha, is buried in Haifa. Both were exiles from Persia, refugees in Ottoman Palestine. The religion they founded today attracts more than five million people from around the world. Adherents see the Baha'i faith as the religion meant for all humanity. As a belief system, it emphasizes the unity of humankind with no regard to racial or cultural barriers. Baha'is see their faith as the religion of peace. They draw on the teaching of Abraham, Buddha, Moses, Zoroaster, Jesus, and Muhammad. All are seen as manifestations of God. The Baha'i religion is yet another faith that calls the Holy Land home.

In addition to being central to the world's three great monotheistic religions—Judaism, Christianity, and Islam—Israel also serves as the spiritual headquarters for the Baha'i faith. Founded in the nineteenth century by Bahá'u'lláh, a native of present-day Iran, the Baha'i religion draws on the teachings of the world's most prominent spiritual leaders. Pictured here is the Shrine of the Bab in Haifa, Israel.

DIVERSITY AMONG ISRAEL'S JEWS

Since A.D. 70, with the Roman destruction of Jerusalem, the world's Jews have lived "in Diaspora." That is, they have lived scattered around the world as minorities in other countries, where they have taken on different languages, philosophies, and interpretations of what it means to be a Jew. As these Diaspora Jews began returning to Palestine during the nineteenth century, they brought a diversity of cultural backgrounds with them. Before World War II, most Jewish immigrants came from Europe, but after the war, the migration streams became ever more diverse. The citizenship laws of Israel, specifically the Law of Return, permit any Jew anywhere in the world to immigrate and become a citizen. Functioning as a secure homeland for the Jewish people, in fact, has been Israel's "reason for being." Israel's first prime minister, David Ben-Gurion, himself from Poland, made that clear: "The supreme aim of the State of Israel is the redemption of the Jewish people, the ingathering of exiles." That aim has been so successfully achieved that more than one-third of the world's 14 million Jews now live in Israel. As a result of this worldwide return migration, Israel's Jewish population represents a diversity of cultures and languages. When observing an English class at Beit Hinuch Tikhon Ironi Gimel in Jerusalem in the late 1990s, a visitor asked students where their parents came from. Six students had at least one parent from Russia, but look at how many other countries are represented below:

Russia	6
Israel	5
Poland	5
Austria	2
Germany	2
Iraq	2
Iran	2
United States	2

Argentina	1
Bulgaria	1
Czech Republic	1
England	1
France	1
Hungary	1
Mozambique	1
Romania	1
Tunisia	1
Yemen	1

The first Jewish immigrants to Israel were the *Ashkenazim* (from the Hebrew word for Germany) from Central Europe. Only after World War II were they followed by the *Sephardim* (from the Hebrew word for Spain), those who have roots in Spain, where they lived until the late 1400s, when they were expelled by fanatic Christians. As these words are used today, Ashkenazim refers to any Jew of European origin, and Sephardim refers to any Jew of "Oriental" origin, that is from Africa or Asia. The Ashkenazim spoke Yiddish. The Sephardim and Oriental Jews spoke Ladino or Arabic.

After the war of 1948–1949, mass immigration from the Arab World, Turkey, and Iran swelled the Jewish population of Israel. By 1960, virtually the entire Jewish population of Yemen, Libya, and Iraq had been resettled in Israel. The most recent large migration, beginning in the late 1980s, has come from the former Soviet Union—Ukraine, Russia, and Belarus, in particular. They came speaking Russian, which is heard today throughout Israel. Another large migration originated in Ethiopia. In 1985 and 1991, the Ethiopians were airlifted to Israel, whisked out of a country beset by political turmoil and famine. Known as the *Felashas,* these African Jews had survived in the mountains of Ethiopia, and their religion evolved in almost total isolation from world Judaism. Beginning in 2002, about 6,000 economically distressed Argentine Jews also took advantage of their right to claim Israeli citizenship. They were escaping the economic collapse of Argentina. The table below illustrates the diversity of the Israeli population.

ISRAELI CITIZENS BORN ABROAD

Former USSR (Russia, Ukraine, Belarus, etc.)	907,200
Morocco	167,400
Romania	125,800
Poland	83,300
Iraq	76,800
North America	69,500
Ethiopia	56,300
Iran	51,600
Algeria/Tunisia	42,300
Yemen	37,000
Other countries	340,500

(Source: *Newsweek,* April 1, 2002, p. 38)

LINGUISTIC DIVERSITY

How would it be possible to unite a nation of Jews if they all spoke different languages? Even before there was an independent State of Israel, that question occupied the minds of Zionist leaders. One of those leaders was named Eliezar Ben Yehuda (1858–1922). In the early twentieth century, there were only 50,000 Jews living in Palestine. Half came from Europe, and most spoke Yiddish, a Jewish language built on a German base. The other half had been born in Ottoman-controlled

Palestine and spoke Arabic, or a dialect called Judeo-Arabic. Ben Yehuda, a specialist in the study of language, recognized that national unity would never materialize if families coming to Israel could not communicate with one another, so he began the process of updating the ancient Hebrew language, the language of the Jewish scriptures. In the words of Eliezar Ben Yehuda in the *Hebrew Language Dictionary*:

> Just as the Jews cannot really become a living nation other than through their return to the land of the Fathers, so too, they are not able to become a living nation other than through their return to the language of the Fathers.

At that time, Hebrew was almost a dead language, but its archaic form was still used in worship. Unfortunately, ancient Hebrew had no words for modern concepts and inventions. Ben Yehuda devised new words from ancient roots and compiled them, along with traditional vocabulary, into a dictionary of modern Hebrew.

Not everyone was happy with the choice of Hebrew. Some considered it a sacred language, too sacred to use on the street. They preferred Yiddish, the most widely spoken tongue prior to independence. Ben Yehuda understood why Yiddish, the Jewish language of Europe, was favored by the Ashkenazi Jews. But he knew that Jews would be returning to Israel from other lands as well. After 1948, Ben Yehuda's investment in the language paid off as Jews from the Spanish-, Arabic-, and English-speaking realms migrated to their newly independent homeland. The first thing they did was learn Hebrew. Their first few weeks in Israel were spent in *ulpanim*, Hebrew-language schools for adults. Hebrew became a tool of nation building. Yiddish, spoken by 12 million people before World War II, went into a tailspin. Now, in Israel (and the United States), there is a Yiddish revival movement. Part of the stimulus has been Israel's many recent Russian immigrants. The older ones had spoken Yiddish in their youth (but had switched to Russian). Now as seniors newly arrived in their "promised land," Yiddish enables them to speak immediately to Jews of the same generation—Jews from Romania, Poland, and Germany. You may know some Yiddish words, for example:

bagel	ring-shaped roll
kibbitz	to meddle
klutz	clumsy person
lox	smoked salmon
shlep	drag

Today, Israel has two official languages, Hebrew and Arabic. Both are Semitic languages, descended from a common ancestor, so they share many of the same sounds and even the same roots. For instance, *shalom* means "peace." It is also used to say both "hello" and "good-bye." *Salaam*, in Arabic, means "peace," and it is also used as part of the traditional greeting. In some parts of Israel, signs appear in both languages. Arabic was the sole language of Palestine until the Zionist migration began. It remains the language of preference among Arab Israelis. English is also widespread, because it has emerged as the global *lingua franca*, which is a language that serves the necessity for communicating among people who speak different languages. Other tongues are heard as well, particularly Russian.

The Russians brought not only their language, but also a different alphabet, the Cyrillic alphabet. It joined the Hebrew, Arabic, and Roman alphabets to make Israel one of the most alphabetically diverse countries in the entire world. If you add the Japanese alphabet, which you see frequently because there are so many Japanese tourists, the alphabet soup gets even thicker. Additional alphabets are used by various Christian sects in Israel. Greek is still used as a liturgical (or church) language in

Greek Orthodox churches, even though their members are Arabic-speaking. Syriac, also known as Aramaic (the language of Jesus), is still used as a liturgical language in Syrian Christian churches. Both have alphabets of their own. Non-Arab Christian groups brought other languages and other alphabets to the Holy Land. The Armenians have maintained Armenian as a living language and use both it and their unique alphabet at home as well as in their schools and churches. The Ethiopian Christians use the Ge'ez language and Ge'ez alphabet in their churches. In fact, Israel is like an alphabet museum with exhibits dating back 2,000 years.

THE WORLD'S CALENDARS

Israel is also a country where at least three different calendars meet and greet arriving tourists. The calendar used by most of the world today is the Christian calendar. It was adopted by Pope Gregory XIII in 1582, by which time the old Julian calendar was out of sync with the seasons. The Gregorian calendar's starting point is the birth of Jesus. Before his birth, dates are reckoned as "Before Christ" (B.C.). After his birth, dates are reckoned as "Anno Domini" (A.D.), or "the year of our Lord." The Christian Gregorian calendar is solar; it is tied to the cycles of the sun. That means that equinoxes and solstices always occur in the same month.

Two other calendars—the Jewish and Muslim—are also in evidence in Israel. Muslims begin counting years from the time that Muhammad fled Mecca and took up residence in Medina. That flight is known as the *hijra*. Consquently, dates are reckoned as A.H., meaning "Anno Hijra," or the year of the Hijra. A.D. 622 marks year one on the Hijri calendar. Muslims, however, favor a lunar month of about 29 days. Consequently, the Muslim calendar year is shorter by about 11 days than the Christian year.

Jews have their own calendar. It is a cross between the lunar calendar and the solar calendar. Jewish years are numbered since creation (a date that is calculated using their scriptures), and a year may have either 12 or 13 months, the thirteenth month being used like a leap year in the Gregorian calendar. The year A.D. 2006 corresponds to the year 5766 in the Jewish calendar and the year 1427 A.H. in the Hijri calendar. Even time differs from group to group in Israel, a land of diversity on every front.

CHAPTER

5

Politics and Government

Israel came into being in 1948, only a few years after the end of World War II. The international boundaries it started with, however, are not the boundaries that define the state today. In fact, twenty-first-century Israel includes almost twice as much territory as the United Nations (UN) had in mind when Israel was created out of the British Mandate of Palestine. As it expanded over the two decades following independence, Israel came to encompass more of the local Arab population, people who call themselves Palestinians. Today, Israel is really two countries in one. There is the State of Israel, and there are the Palestinian Territories. The Territories are known to the world as the West Bank and Gaza Strip. Fragmented parts of the territories have been known since 1993 as the Palestinian Autonomy, an evolving self-governing, perhaps independent, homeland.

The Palestinian Territories comprise about 22 percent of Israel's total area. Israel itself has final authority over the territories. Within the Palestinian Territories, however, there is a "homeland" in the process of being born. It is called the Palestinian Autonomy. Also, within the territories are Jews, whose settlements operate as if they were fully part of the State of Israel. In Hebron, a city of 120,000 Palestinians, for instance, there is a settlement of only 450 Jews. The map of Israel as a whole is like a jigsaw puzzle in which the pieces overlap. The Palestinian Autonomy makes the West Bank and Gaza resemble a piece of Swiss cheese; it exists in fragments too numerous to count. In these fragments, Palestinians are responsible for civil affairs, internal security, and public order. If it were a cartographic jigsaw puzzle, it would be difficult to put together.

Israel was founded as a "homeland" for the Jewish people; it is recognized by most other countries in the world and has a seat in the UN (since 1949). The Palestinian Autonomy is self-governing, but it is not independent. It was established as a "homeland" for the Palestinian people. Palestinians would like to become totally independent, but the Israelis do not want that to happen. The Israelis want the Palestinians to be satisfied with "home government" instead of a fully independent "homeland." They have been willing to give Palestinians authority to make many of their own decisions in areas of daily life, but Israelis are unwilling to see Palestinians on a par with other independent states in the world. For one thing, it might mean the Palestinians would build an army, make defense alliances with other Arab states, and threaten Israel. How did such an irresolvable conflict arise? Its roots are in the rule of the Ottoman Empire before and British Empire after World War I.

A political entity called the British Mandate of Palestine preceded Israel on the map of the Middle East. It had basically the same boundaries as Israel does today (with the West Bank and Gaza, but without the Golan Heights). After World War I, the British were given control of the territory by the League of Nations (the organization that preceded the United Nations). They held it in trust for more than two decades. After 1945, however, the British were eager to get rid of their overseas possessions and devote their energies to recovering from a long and devastating war. The newly formed UN, therefore, took on the responsibility of deciding how to end the mandate. But, there was a problem. Two groups of people wanted the same tract of land. In fact, both groups wanted all of what had been the British mandate. Both the Jews and the Palestinian Arabs believed that they had been promised the land by the British.

The basis of Jewish claims was grounded in two factors. First, the Balfour Declaration was issued by the British Government in 1917. It stated:

> His Majesty's Government view with favour the establishment in Palestine of a national home for the Jewish people, and will use their best endeavours to facilitate the achievement of this object, it being clearly understood that nothing shall be done which may prejudice the civil and religious rights of existing non-Jewish communities in Palestine, or the rights and political status enjoyed by Jews in any other country.

The Balfour Declaration ensured that Britain would stand behind the creation of a "Jewish home." The idea of a homeland was the outcome of the Zionist movement in Europe, a Jewish nationalist movement. Zionism, however, was not a religious movement; its founders were secular Jews, full of nationalistic, but not religious, zeal.

The second basis of Jewish claims to the land was the reality of what was happening in Palestine. The population mix there was changing. Beginning in the mid-1800s, while the Ottoman Turks were still in control, Jews had begun to return to the region. A few settled on the outskirts of Jerusalem. Their settlement overlooked Jaffa Gate. It was created to help relieve crowding and poverty in the Old City. Today, it is known as Yemin Moshe. Most of those who arrived, however, chose to live in the sandy coastal area north of Jaffa, whose harbor had been the "gateway to the Holy Land" since ancient times. New immigrants, sometimes with the help of the Jewish National Fund, bought land from the local Arab population and began to farm it. These Jaffa suburbs, begun in 1909, were to become the city of Tel Aviv. The immigrant streams from Europe grew larger under the British. It was not long until Tel Aviv was the most populous city in Israel, and new communities began to develop along the coast north and south of Tel Aviv. European Jews were acting out their Zionist ambitions with full British approval.

The British, however, had also made promises to the Arab people of the region. Prior to the British mandate, almost all of the lands of southwest Asia were under the control of the sprawling Ottoman Empire with its capital at Istanbul (now in Turkey). Early in World War I, the Ottoman Empire decided to ally itself with Germany. Britain (and other powers) knew it had to defeat Germany and its allies, including the Ottomans. To do that, the British Crown made alliances with the Arabs of the Arabian Peninsula and the eastern Mediterranean. British soldiers (Lawrence of Arabia being the best known) promised the Arabs that if they helped the British throw the Ottomans out of Arab lands, the Arabs would once again rule themselves. Instead, after the "Great War" resulted in the defeat of Germany and the end of the Ottoman Empire, most of the Arabs were put under the sovereignty of Great Britain or France, both of which were given pieces of southwest Asia as mandates. In addition to feeling cheated, the Palestinians remembered the second half of the Balfour Declaration: "nothing shall be done which may prejudice the civil and religious rights of existing non-Jewish communities in Palestine."

The stage was thus set for conflict and war. The first four decades of the twentieth century saw repeated skirmishes, terrorist attacks, and demonstrations that involved Jews, Arabs, and, after 1922, the British. Right through World War II, no one was satisfied with the status quo in the Middle East. And at the time, no one could envision a future that would be satisfactory to all of the different peoples and outside powers that were involved in the region. At this point, responsibility was turned over to the fledgling United Nations.

The UN knew it had to end British rule over its mandate, Palestine. The organization had already declared the need for a new political map based on the goal of "self-determination" for all peoples. The independence movement was spreading; ending colonialism was the order of the day. With that in mind, the UN Partition Plan of 1947 was devised. It envisioned a "two-state" solution to the problem of two peoples with conflicting ambitions to control the same land. The plan called for a state comprising about 60 percent of Palestine for the Jews, and another state comprising about 40 percent of Palestine for the Arabs. In this plan, Jerusalem would have become an independent, international city belonging to neither state. Both states would have had an unusual shape, and neither side liked the proposed boundaries. But the Palestinians believed that they had gotten the worst deal. They had a majority of the population, but would get only a minority of the land. Their state also would have been divided into three separate parts, with small strips of the Jewish state separating the parts. It would be a small, fragmented state and would not include the third-holiest Muslim site in the world, the Dome of the Rock in Jerusalem. Not only did the Palestinians take offense, so did the rest of the Arab World.

Israel gained independence on May 14, 1948, under the UN Partition Plan. Six Arab states invaded the next day in an effort to remove Israel from the map as an independent entity. That was the first Arab-Israeli war. Even though the Jews were outnumbered, the war resulted in large territorial gains for the State of Israel, including a corridor of land to Jerusalem and all of Galilee in the north. It did not result in the creation of an independent Palestine. Instead, fragments of what the UN envisioned as Palestine came under the control of neighboring Arab states. The West Bank, including the walled city of Jerusalem, became part of Transjordan, which then changed its name to Jordan. The Gaza Strip became part of Egypt. The rest of what was to become an independent Palestine became part of the State of Israel. The war of 1948–49 is known as the "War of Independence" among Israelis. Among Palestinians, it is known as "al nakba," the catastrophe. Arabs were outraged. Not only had Israel made substantial territorial gains, but most of the Palestinian population had been forced out of their homes and villages to become refugees in neighboring countries.

The borders established by the armistice of 1949 held until 1967. In that year, Israel gained even more territory. In response to aggressive actions by Egypt and Syria, Israel launched an invasion of the Sinai Peninsula, the West Bank, and the Golan Heights. From Egypt, it seized the Gaza Strip and the entire Sinai right up to the Suez Canal. It defeated the Jordanian Army to acquire the West Bank and, most importantly, the holy city of Jerusalem. It also captured the Golan Heights from Syria. Neither the Sinai nor the Golan had been part of the Mandate of Palestine, and neither of them had a Palestinian population. Bedouin Arabs lived in the Sinai, and Syrian Arabs (and Druze) lived in the Golan. All of these areas became "occupied territories."

One occupied territory, the Sinai, was given back to Egypt in 1982. Another, the Golan (minus a small strip turned back to Syria), was annexed to Israel in 1981, despite objections by the UN and in the face of Syrian wrath. The remaining two, the West Bank and Gaza, became territories with an ambiguously defined political existence. Were they "occupied territories" in the sense that they were occupied by the Israeli military? Could they be called "colonies" of Israel, since Jews came to colonize and solidify control over the land? Should they just become a full and official part of the State of Israel, an Arab part with representation in the Israeli parliament? Should they be given self-governing rights or full independence? These are questions

The area defined as the West Bank, which forms part of the Palestinian Territories in Israel, has long been ambiguous. Pictured here is the security barrier that divides Jerusalem from the West Bank village of Abu Dis. The security barrier between the two settlements was redrawn in 2005, because it had disrupted many Palestinian settlements.

that since 1967 have still not been answered. Today, the State of Israel and the Palestinian Territories are governed under two different regimes, only one of which is fully sovereign.

GOVERNMENT OF THE STATE OF ISRAEL

The State of Israel (not including the Palestinian Territories) functions under a system of government called a parliamentary democracy. The 120-member Israeli Parliament is called the Knesset. The head of government and chief executive officer of the state is the prime minister. The head of state, the president, is elected by the Knesset. Israel also has an independent national court system that includes both secular and religious courts. Israel's Supreme Court, however, has limited rights of "judicial review": It does not have the power of the U.S. Supreme Court in deciding whether or not laws are constitutional.

The Knesset is an elected assembly in which issues are debated, positions taken, and laws enacted. Citizens of Israel may vote their party preference in determining who serves in the Knesset. Palestinians on the West Bank and Gaza do not vote because they are not citizens. The Israeli settlers in the West Bank do vote because they are Israeli citizens. Settlers in the Gaza Strip did vote until their settlements were taken down in 2005. Seats in the Knesset are allocated on the basis of party strength, and the political party with the most seats puts together a coalition government.

During the course of Israeli history since independence, more than three dozen political parties have been formed. Not all have survived. The two major parties are the Labor Party (more liberal) and the Likud Party (more conservative), but neither has had enough strength to govern alone. Instead, coalitions have had to be formed by inviting smaller parties into the government. These smaller parties are often formed along ethnic or religious lines. The process of coalition building gives the small political parties more power than their vote strength might warrant. One of the best-known minority parties is called Shas. It is made up of North African Jews who came to Israel after 1948 and found that their interests were not being represented by either the Labor Party or the Likud Party, both of which were solidly in the hands of European Jews. The most recent party to take form is Kadima ("forward"). It was started by Ariel Sharon as a centrist alternative to Likud, the party that Sharon led to victory in the Knesset elections of 2003. In the

Knesset elections of 2006, Kadima won more seats than any other party, but not a majority. It was able to govern by forming a coalition with Labor and several smaller parties.

Since the elections of 1996, voters have directly elected the prime minister. The prime minister and his or her Cabinet of Ministers comprise the supreme executive authority of the state. He or she has powers comparable to the U.S. president. The prime minister and the members of the Knesset are elected for four-year terms, but a "vote of no confidence" on an important piece of legislation may lead to new elections at any time. Israel has had some famous prime ministers over the course of its existence:

David Ben-Gurion (1948–1953; 1955–1963)

Moshe Sharett (1954–1955)

Levi Eshkol (1963–1969)

Golda Meir (1969–1974)

Yitzhak Rabin (1974–1977; 1992–1995)

Menachem Begin (1977–1983)

Yitzhak Shamir (1983–1984; 1986–1992)

Shimon Peres (1984–1986; 1995–1996)

Benjamin Netanyahu (1996–1999)

Ehud Barak (1999–2000)

Ariel Sharon (2000–2006)

Ehud Olmert (2006–)

David Ben-Gurion is revered today as the "father of Israeli statehood." He worked tirelessly, and ruthlessly, to rid Palestine of the British. He, like many other early prime ministers, had been part of the Haganah, the terrorist band that confronted the British. Israel's international airport, located eight miles from his house in Tel Aviv, is named after him.

Golda Meir was prime minister during the Yom Kippur War of 1973. She was Israel's first, and to this day only, woman to hold the office. Meir was born in Ukraine, but migrated to the United States in 1906. Later, she became a schoolteacher in Milwaukee. In 1921, while in her 20s, she made alliyah to Israel. There she was destined eventually to serve 10 years as foreign minister and five years as prime minister, one of the first women prime ministers in the world.

Menachem Begin, the first Likud prime minister, signed a peace treaty with Egypt in 1979. The signing ceremony took place at the White House, where he and Egyptian President Anwar Sadat were guests of President Jimmy Carter. Begin was born in czarist Russia. His parents lost their lives in Nazi concentration camps during World War II. He, himself, was imprisoned in Siberian labor camps by Joseph Stalin.

Yitzhak Rabin, a native of Jerusalem, did more than any other prime minister to resolve problems with the Palestinians. While he was prime minister, the Oslo Accords put the Palestinians on the road to self-government. In 1994, he signed a historic peace treaty with Jordan, which normalized relations between the two countries. That same year, along with Yasser Arafat and Shimon Peres, Rabin received the Nobel Peace Prize. In 1995, he signed an "interim agreement on the West Bank and Gaza Strip," which is also known as Oslo II. U.S. President Bill Clinton was instrumental in helping to facilitate these diplomatic triumphs. On November 4, 1995, Rabin was assassinated by an Israeli extremist. An eternal flame burns today on the street in Tel Aviv where his life ended.

Ariel Sharon, who was born in an agricultural village (moshav) in central Israel, presided over one of the darkest periods in modern Israeli history, a period of Palestinian uprisings and suicide bombings, and a period of brutal repression of the Palestinians by the Israeli Army. For a time,

Prime Minister Ehud Olmert, left, shakes hands with President Moshe Katsav shortly after the swearing-in ceremony of the new Israeli government in May 2006. Olmert, Israel's twelfth prime minister, replaced Ariel Sharon, who suffered a severe hemorrhagic stroke in early January 2006.

any pretense of self-government by the Palestinians came to an end. Then, in 2004, Sharon announced his intentions to withdraw Israeli settlements in the Gaza Strip. He had come to the conclusion that the settlements were a security burden and a source of continuous friction. By 2005, they were gone, but early in 2006, Sharon suffered a massive stroke from which he never recovered.

Ehud Olmert became Israel's twelfth prime minister in 2006, after serving as deputy prime minister under Ariel Sharon. Before that, for a decade, he served as mayor of Jerusalem. Olmert's grandfather fled Russia after World War I and settled in China, where his father grew up. Ehud Olmert, however, was born in Israel. He was only two years old when Israel gained independence.

Since 1950, Jerusalem has been the official capital city of Israel. Tel Aviv was the first capital. Under the UN Partition Plan of 1947, Jerusalem was to be under international jurisdiction. During the 1948–1949 war, however, Israeli troops drove into the Judean Hills and entered the Old City. The Israelis could not hold Jerusalem, however. After the war, it (and the entire West Bank) became a part of the Hashemite Kingdom of Jordan. Nevertheless, the new, expanded Israeli State controlled West Jerusalem all the way up to a demilitarized zone that separated the new Jewish state from the Old City. With little dissension, the Israelis decided that the national government would be transferred to Jerusalem from Tel Aviv. The international community was less enthusiastic about the move. To this day, most embassies remain in Tel Aviv. It is there that the U.S. Embassy overlooks the Mediterranean Sea.

GOVERNMENT OF THE PALESTINIAN TERRITORIES

Today, Israel includes a fledgling state within a state, the Palestinian Autonomy, incorporating much of the West Bank and Gaza Strip. Autonomy, in this sense, means a self-governing state. In reality, however, the Palestinian Autonomy operates under the authority of Israel, which has permitted it to develop the trappings of statehood. It has a flag of its own, postage stamps, its own school system, citizenship rights, its own passports, a government structure, tourist police, taxing authority, and observer status at the UN. What it does not have is independence; neither is it permitted to develop a military force. By 2000, the Palestinian Autonomy included about 40 percent of the West Bank and Gaza, but the territory existed in dozens of pieces that did not border one another.

The government of the Palestinian people in the West Bank and Gaza is in the hands of the Palestinian Authority. It began as a government in exile when Yasser Arafat, a Palestinian

Muslim, pushed a declaration of independence through the Palestinian National Council, during its meeting in Algeria in November 1988. The idea of an independent Palestine was really born much earlier, however, when the Palestine Liberation Organization (PLO) was founded in 1964. Arafat became chairman of the PLO in 1969, and terrorism against the Israelis came to characterize the 1970s and 1980s. Early in the 1990s, however, better relationships began to develop between Israelis and Palestinians. The PLO's headquarters moved from Tunis, where it had operated in exile, to the West Bank and Gaza in 1994, a year after Palestine recognized the State of Israel, and Israel recognized the PLO as the legitimate representative of the Palestinian people. Yasser Arafat held the chairmanship of the PLO until his death in 2004.

An interim Palestinian government began operating in 1994 as portions of the West Bank and Gaza were handed over to the Palestinian Authority. The interim government was an outcome of the Israeli-PLO Agreements of 1993. In the first elections held in 1996, three-fourths of the Palestinian people voted, and Yasser Arafat was elected president of the Palestinian Authority by a decisive majority. Members of Arafat's Fatah Party were elected to a majority of seats in the Palestinian Legislative Council. The power of the Palestinian Authority and its geographical range continued to expand until the outbreak of the second intifadah in 2000. After Arafat's death, Mahmoud Abbas, himself a refugee of the 1948 war, was elected president of the Palestinian Authority. In the region, he is best known as Abu Mazen, an honorific name that means "father of Mazen." Mazen is his eldest son. Like his predecessor, Abu Mazen is a member of the Fatah party.

The Palestinian Legislative Council meets in the West Bank town of Ramallah. It also has an assembly building in Gaza. Because the Palestinian Autonomy exists in two separate parts, with Israel in between, it is sometimes impossible for the council's members to convene in one place. Some of them are not

Mahmoud Abbas, left, is pictured here with former Palestine Liberation Organization (PLO) leader Yasser Arafat, shortly before Arafat's death in 2004. Abbas was elected president of the Palestinian National Authority (PNA) in January 2005 and has pursued peaceful relations with Israel.

permitted on Israeli soil because of their terrorist connections. Videoconferencing is often used to hold legislative assemblies. In 2006, free elections to the Council were held for the first time in a decade. The party of Yasser Arafat and Mahmoud Abbas, the Fatah party, lost its majority in those elections. A party called Hamas won 76 of the 132 parliamentary seats. Hamas is formally known as the Islamic Resistance Movement. It does not accept the existence of Israel, a state that it wants to erase from the map. Hamas favors a one-state solution to the Arab-Israeli conflict; it favors the creation of a state called Palestine to replace Israel. That objective complicates the peace process that has been aiming toward a "two-state solution": a state for Israelis and a state for Palestinians. The Palestinian Authority now operates under a divided government: The presidency is in the hands of the moderate Fatah party and the Legislative Council is in the hands of the radical Hamas party.

Thus, Israeli Jews and Palestinian Arabs continue their political battles over who should reign supreme in the land between the Mediterranean Sea and the Jordan River. There is constant tension between the two. That tension has taken the form of wars, uprisings, military occupations, and terrorism. Israel is currently trying to unilaterally resolve the conflict by building a wall, or separation barrier, between the State of Israel and the West Bank. Construction of the wall was begun in 2002 at the height of the Al Aqsa Intifadah to stop Palestinian suicide bombers from crossing the border into Israel. The same strategy seemed to have worked in the 1990s, when the Gaza Strip was separated from Israel by a wall. The barrier around Gaza, however, followed the 1967 armistice line; the West Bank wall does not. It cuts into Palestinian territory, putting about 15 percent of the West Bank on the Israeli side of the barrier. From Israel's perspective, the security fences around the Gaza Strip and the West Bank have been successful in reducing terrorist attacks on Israelis. From the Palestinians' perspective, the wall makes them prisoners in their own home, limits their economic prospects, and deprives them of even more territory. What the walls around the Palestinian Territories really mean, however, is that Israel and the Palestinians will grow further apart rather than closer together. It is the sign of a divorce. Whether the political gulf between the two peoples will be narrowed by diplomacy or widened by war remains to be seen.

6

Israel's Economy

Within Israel are two economies operating within sight of each other: the economy of the Israelis and that of the Palestinians. The line that divides the State of Israel from the Palestinian Territories resembles the divide between the world's developed economies ("the rich world") and the developing economies ("the poor world"). The per-capita income of Israel is about $24,000. In the Palestinian Territories, however, it is only about $1,500 and in the Gaza Strip far less. Half the Palestinian population lives below the poverty line. The Palestinians who are doing the best economically are those who are Israeli citizens, the Arab Israelis. Despite its lack of oil, Israel is one of the richest countries in the Middle East. It also ranks higher than any country in eastern Europe and higher than some countries in southern Europe in its economic strength.

Prior to the second intifadah, the contrast between the developed and less developed sides of Israel was nowhere more evident than in

Jerusalem, a city divided. From the West Bank, Palestinian women wearing heavily embroidered clothing would bring burlap bags (now more often made of plastic) of produce to the plaza outside Damascus Gate, in the heart of Arab East Jerusalem. They would spread their bounty on the ground and stay until it was sold. Their sales were part of the informal economy, unsanctioned by the government. They sold fruits and vegetables, or even mass-produced household items and clothing; what they earned would go back to the West Bank to enrich the economy there. Anything for children would always sell well, and the reason was clear: Palestinians have large families, and the women of Damascus Gate would bring their children with them. Young Palestinians from the West Bank simply added to the many boys and girls who already lived in and around the Old City. The children mixed freely with adults, ran errands, and helped their parents. Around Damascus Gate, the age structure of the Palestinian population was apparent: half were under 18 years of age. Now, Palestinian men, women, and children find it difficult to cross from the West Bank into Jerusalem.

Only a short walk separates Damascus Gate from Ben Yehuda Street in the heart of Jewish West Jerusalem. Around Damascus Gate, you see only Palestinians (and tourists). Along Ben Yehuda, you see only Jews (and tourists). At Damascus Gate, you bargain and barter for what you want—a practice typical of traditional economies. On Ben Yehuda, you pay fixed, usually high, prices. There is even a multilevel, enclosed shopping mall, plus numerous franchises and lots of landscaping. Europeans and Americans feel at home in West Jerusalem, because it is the retailing environment they know. The one thing not found in West Jerusalem is a single Palestinian. They are not recognizable by their physical features; rather, they are identifiable by their clothes, mannerisms, and even haircuts (and, of course, their language). Anyone who seems to be from East Jerusalem may be

The Damascus Gate area of Old Jerusalem is predominately Palestinian and is home to one of the city's largest markets. Unlike the neighboring shops on Ben Yehuda Street, the shops in the Damascus Gate area permit patrons to barter for goods, instead of paying a fixed price.

stopped and required to produce identification. Economically and demographically, East Jerusalem and West Jerusalem are a world apart.

Unfortunately, more than one out of three working-age adults in the Palestinian Territories do not hold a job because of the weak economy. Even in Israel, the 1.5 million immigrants that have arrived over the past two decades have had a difficult time finding jobs. Fortunately, many Jews from the former Soviet Union came with skills. The Soviet educational system excelled in the natural sciences and the arts. Those skills are now being put to work in building the high-tech sector of the Israeli economy (for example, in computers, electronics, and biotechnology) and contributing to the country's quality of life (orchestras and theater companies).

Ethiopian Jews, the Falashas, came during the same time period as the Russians (although in smaller numbers), but they arrived with little formal education. Nevertheless, they have provided much manual labor, something that every economy needs. And their children are getting the education they never could have received in Ethiopia. Unfortunately, from the Palestinian perspective, the Ethiopians are getting an education that most Palestinians could only dream of for their children. Nevertheless, within the Arab World, the Palestinian people are comparatively well educated, and many attend universities in the West Bank or abroad, some even in Israel. Given the weak Palestinian economy, however, when they finish their education, they cannot find jobs equal to their talents, or receive the salaries they expect. These graduates are among those who believe that an independent Palestine would be better off economically.

NATURAL RESOURCES AND AGRICULTURE

Neither Israel nor the Palestinian Territories is rich in natural resources. There is not enough fresh water, and only a few valuable mineral and energy resources exist. As Golda Meir supposedly once noted: "Moses dragged us through the desert to the one place in the Middle East where there is no oil." Only recently has natural gas been discovered in the Mediterranean Sea off the coast of Ashquelon in Israel and the Gaza Strip. Israelis hope that this natural gas and some small oil deposits will make them less dependent on imported energy resources. The discovery also adds to the development potential of the Palestinian Territories. Today oil is imported from non-Arab countries, including the United Kingdom and Mexico, and coal from Australia and South Africa.

Other natural resources include limestone from the hills of Judea and Samaria and marble from the Galilee region. Israel is lucky to have such fine building stone. The walls and structures of Jerusalem have been erected from local limestone resources, giving the city a golden hue that sets it apart from others. Salts (bromine and magnesium) from the Dead Sea and small deposits of phosphates and copper are the only other mineral resources of value.

Only 2 percent of the Israeli population and 13 percent of the Palestinian population continues to be engaged in farming, the most important of the primary economic activities. Nevertheless, food and food processing remain important to both economies. The traditional mixed-crop and livestock farming of the Mediterranean Basin is often called "Mediterranean agriculture." It makes the most of scarce water resources by depending on plants and animals that thrive under drier conditions. Crops that dominate Mediterranean agriculture are well known throughout the world: wheat, tree fruit (especially citrus), olives, and grapes. Sheep and goats take advantage of the drier, more rugged terrain. Fish from the Mediterranean and the Sea of Galilee, home of the tilapia known as St. Peter's fish, have traditionally supplemented the food supply.

Wheat grown in Mediterranean climates is winter wheat. It is planted in the fall and grows during the mild winter, which is also the rainy season. Of the crops that can be grown in Israel and for which there is a market, wheat has the lowest value. That is why Israel has devoted its land to the production of higher-value crops and has chosen to import most wheat. Olive trees are well adapted to the Mediterranean, because they are suited to seasonally dry conditions. Their fruit, the olive, is not juicy (hence, does not require much water); its leaves are small and waxy (retarding moisture loss); and its roots go deep into the soil (giving it access to water). The Galilee region and the Judean Hills are covered with olive groves. Olives are easily preserved for year-round consumption, they are high in energy value, and olive trees keep producing year after year for centuries. Investment in an olive grove is an investment for life; the olive has become the symbol of life in Mediterranean lands and is a part of every meal. Olive oil is used for cooking and for

Olives are native to Israel and are one of the country's primary agricultural crops. Olive trees, such as the ones pictured here near Galilee, can survive in poor soil and live for hundreds of years.

manufacturing soap. "Palm*olive*" is a brand name that commemorates the importance of olive oil to the soap industry.

Grapes are well suited to the Mediterranean climate as well, but their cultivation had all but died out during Ottoman times. Because Muslims are not permitted to consume alcohol, there was little demand for wine. When Israel was established, grapes again became part of the agricultural landscape. Today Israel produces some very good wines, and growing grapes has emerged as one of the main agricultural activities of the Golan Heights since 1967. Other types of fruit are also a part of

Israel's Mediterranean landscape, especially citrus fruits, pomegranates, and figs. Today, most of these are destined for domestic consumption.

The Jordan River valley, with its near-tropical climate and year-round growing season, is almost perfect for growing many of these crops, plus bananas, where water is available for irrigation. Dates, an oasis crop, are also important agricultural commodities in the Jordan and Arava valleys. Thanks to modern technology, an extinct species of date palm was brought back to life in 2005. A 2,000-year-old seed, found in archeological excavations at Masada, germinated and gave life to a palm tree on Kitura kibbutz just north of Aqaba. It is the oldest tree seed that has ever sprouted. Dates (used to make "honey"), along with pomegranates, figs, olives, grapes, barley, and wheat, came to symbolize the bounty of nature in the ancient Fertile Crescent. They are mentioned in the Bible as the "seven species."

Some nontraditional crops also have become important moneymakers. Cotton, for fiber and cottonseed oil, was introduced to Israel in the 1950s. It must be grown under irrigation. Sugar beets are an important source of sugar. Flowers have become highly valuable commodities grown for the European market. Field crops are grown for livestock, particularly the many dairy and cattle herds. Pastoral agriculture helps the population survive on the drier margins of the Mediterranean world. Goats, a staple of traditional Mediterranean agriculture, are rare today because they are so hard on the land. Sheep, denizens of short grasslands, are found in the West Bank, usually tended by Palestinian children or old men, or perhaps by the very few Bedouin Arabs who still wander the Judean and Negev deserts. Flocks of sheep commonly block the highways of the West Bank as they move from one pasture to another. Lamb and chicken are perhaps the most popular meats in Israel, though the beef industry fills the culinary demands of many immigrants from the United States and Europe. Eating pork, of course, is forbidden by both the Jewish and Islamic faiths.

The successful rural economies of the early immigrants are all the more surprising because most Jews who migrated to Israel during the nineteenth and tweentieth centuries were not farmers. They had lived in the cities of Europe, many confined to ghettos. Nevertheless, almost all began their new life by getting off the boat in Jaffa, the traditional "gateway to Palestine," and heading to the cheap land north of town. It was inexpensive because it was sandy, sometimes waterlogged, and not economically developed. The Arab landlords were happy to sell the land, sometimes to individuals, but more often to the Jewish National Fund, a pool of money put together from contributions of European Jews. The only way for these new immigrants to survive was to farm, so they moved onto the sand-dune frontier, drained the land, and planted crops. Subsistence farming, however, quickly gave way to commercial agriculture. Their first agricultural triumph came in producing citrus fruit for the European market. The Jaffa Orange, named after the port city, became world famous for its high quality. Those early farmers learned to grow other crops as well. This population of Jews eventually grew into the city of Tel Aviv.

The success of these early farmers in developing the sand dunes north of Jaffa taught them how productive a seemingly barren environment could be. Management of resources was the key. Later in the century, the Israelis devoted that same ingenuity to devising new systems of irrigation, systems that would make their scarce water resources go further. Drip irrigation was developed as an alternative to flooding or spraying water over the fields. The challenge was to give each plant only the amount of water it needed to grow. In traditional irrigation systems, most of the water delivered to a field is lost to evaporation. Drip irrigation enables cotton producers, for instance, to "drip" the exact amount of water from a plastic tube onto the ground above each plant's root zone. Today, the whole operation may even be computerized. With water, the dry-land zones of the world, including Israel, have become some of the most productive farmlands. In an arid region, the sun shines all day, unobstructed by cloud cover. Sunshine, together with water and soil nutrients, powers photosynthesis—the keys to plant growth. Too much water, however, can be as bad as aridity. Excess water evaporates, but the salts dissolved in that water stay behind and build up in the soil. Those salts retard plant growth and turn the foliage yellow. Fields may end up looking like salt pans, covered with a thin layer of white salty powder. By minimizing the amount of water distributed to the fields, drip irrigation minimizes the problem of salinity as well: less water equals less salt.

MANUFACTURING AND SERVICES

Few people are needed today in agriculture, fishing, and mining. A few more are needed in the manufacturing sector. Perhaps the best known of Israel's manufactured products are cut and polished diamonds. Rough diamonds are imported, cut, and polished in the workshops of greater Tel Aviv; they are then sold on the world market at a much higher price. Prior to the establishment of Israel, Antwerp, Belgium, had been the diamond-cutting capital of the world. The Jews of Antwerp dominated the business. During World War II and especially after Israeli independence, many of Antwerp's diamond cutters left for Israel and took the industry with them. Today, about half of the world's gem quality cut diamonds originate in Israel.

Today, neither agriculture nor manufacturing dominates the Israeli labor force. The primary activity is the provision of services. Most of those who hold jobs are employed in the tertiary, or service, sector. Three-quarters of the Israeli workforce and one-third of the workers in the Palestinian Territories are employed in services, and the service sector is the most important growth area of both economies. And it is the high-level services connected with biotechnologies, information technologies, communications, and business systems that are growing the fastest. Israel's own "Silicon Valley" is located outside Tel Aviv. The best-known recent product to be invented there is the Centrino chip, marketed by Intel to the world's computer industry. It represents a breakthrough in computer technology, because it uses so much less energy than other chips. Intel itself has had offices in Israel since 1974.

Tourism is also a major industry in Israel, but its fortunes rise and fall in concert with the Arab-Israeli conflict. Jerusalem, however, assures that there will always be a market for tourist-oriented industries in the Holy Land. Nazareth, Jesus's boyhood home, and the Sea of Galilee, are also popular among Christian tourists. In addition to religious sites, Israel offers coastal resorts along the Mediterranean and Dead Sea coasts, and around Eilat on the Gulf of Aqaba. In 2003, Israel's national airline, El Al, went private, but it remains an important component of Israel's tourist industry.

THE ECONOMY OF THE PALESTINIAN TERRITORIES

Within the Palestinian Territories, there are six primary sources of wealth: (1) agriculture and grazing; (2) craft industries, such as making pottery and sandals; (3) service industries for the tourist market; (4) wages brought home from jobs in Israel, especially construction; (5) remittances, the money sent home from Palestinians working in Europe or the oil-rich states; and (6) transfer payments from other Arab states, or from Europeans who often fund improvements in infrastructure or establish clinics. One thing is evident from the list: The Palestinian economy depends heavily on Israel as a source area for tourists, as a market for local agricultural and craft industries, and as a source of jobs in construction.

Consequently, the actions of Israel have a greater impact on the Palestinians than other economic forces. Border crossings between the Palestinian Territories and Israel can be closed at the whim of Israeli authorities. Closures can last from days to months to years. When the borders are closed, Palestinians are unable to get to their jobs in Israel. Thousands of dollars are

Tourism is a major industry in Israel and many vacationers flock to Jerusalem to take in the sites. Here, tourists view the city's skyline from the Mount of Olives (the Dome of the Rock is in the foreground).

consequently lost to the Palestinian economy. The Israeli economy suffers, too. Israelis have no one to do work in construction, or to fill the many low-paying service jobs.

The Palestinians also have been able to take advantage of the demand for Bible-based tourism. The West Bank town of Jericho, including Elisha's spring, is an important place in the Judeo-Christian Old Testament. The New Testament records the birth of Jesus in Bethlehem, his baptism by John in the Jordan River, and his temptation in the wilderness. Each of these events took place in the West Bank. And the last days of Jesus' life on Earth took place on the Mount of Olives (in Arab East Jerusalem) and in the Arab sections of the Old City. The Palestinians have tried to make access to these sites ever easier for international tourists. For instance, a cable car was built to take visitors from Jericho to the Qaranal Monastery (Greek Orthodox), where Jesus was tempted by the devil for 40 days. There are more than a billion Christians in the world, and millions of them visit the Christian sites of Palestine. The newest element of the West Bank tourist economy, however, was designed to expand the tourist market beyond pilgrimage sites. A new casino-hotel was built outside Jericho, designed to appeal to both Israeli and international gamblers. It opened in 1998 and closed at the beginning of the Al Aqsa Intifadah. The cable car to Qaranal also closed for lack of tourists.

THE ECONOMY OF ISRAEL

Today, Israelis are dependent on the free-enterprise system. It was not capitalism, however, that built a nation out of the many streams of Jewish immigrants. It was socialism. The founders of the Zionist movement were European socialists. They thought the interest of the community—not the elite capitalist class—should be first and foremost in importance. At the very foundation of the Israeli economy were two institutions that embodied the principles of socialism: the *kibbutzim*, or rural collectives in which property was owned by the entire community, and the *moshavim*, or rural cooperatives in which property was privately owned. Both were basically farming villages surrounded by fields and pastures, often with small industries attached. The golden age of the kibbutzim is now over, but for decades they defined what it meant to be an Israeli.

The first kibbutz, named Deganiya, was constructed near the Sea of Galilee in 1909. Immigrants at that time were usually destined to spend their lives on kibbutzim. Each resident of the kibbutz had a job to do: some worked in the fields, others in the shops, schools, or laundry. A governing committee assigned both jobs and privileges. The success of the kibbutz was more important than the satisfaction of the individual residents. Rather than earning wages, residents received an allowance. Profits went to the kibbutz. There were separate cottages for adults and children. People ate in communal dining halls, rather than in private dining rooms. Some kibbutzim had a communal car, the use of which could be requested from the governing committee. If someone wanted to go to college, the kibbutz would have to agree. Even clothing was community property in the early days. Dirty clothes went to the laundry and clean clothes came back—not to private dresser drawers, but to clothes closets used by all. Communism and socialism can be defined as systems in which wealth is allocated "from each according to his ability, to each according to his needs." In Israel, a true form of Communism worked, but it worked on a small scale and only for a short period of time.

For a generation now, it has been hard to keep young people on the kibbutz. They want to live in Tel Aviv, Haifa, or Jerusalem. Older teens want to have paying jobs and a car of their own. They want to make decisions themselves. Yet, the kibbutzim have not disappeared; they have simply changed. Kibbutzim now specialize in marketable commodities, host tourists, and operate more like for-profit businesses. There is even a Christian kibbutz. Nevertheless, the kibbutz of old holds a special place in the hearts of the Israelis. In fact, there were really only two institutions that forged an Israeli nation out of a ragtag assortment of immigrants: the kibbutz and the military. They were the stuff of which legends were made.

WHAT'S FOR BREAKFAST?

When you eat an Israeli breakfast today, you are affirming the lasting impact of the kibbutz on but one aspect of national culture. An Israeli breakfast is big and fresh from the farm—that is, fresh from the kibbutz. A typical breakfast includes eggs (perhaps with cheese or mushrooms), olives, greens, tomatoes, cucumbers, spring onions, peppers, sour cream, bread, butter, fruit jam, orange juice, and coffee or tea. With the exception of the last two, these represent the bounty of the kibbutz. They are an affirmation of what determination and a little water can coax out of a dry environment. (Note the absence of bacon or sausage, since pork is forbidden by Jewish law.)

A traditional Palestinian breakfast, and one that is typical of the Arab realm of Asia, consists of fuul, khobz, and very sweet tea (or perhaps coffee). Fuul is a hot, thick soup made of fava beans (broad beans) and lentils mashed into a chunky paste. It is seasoned and topped with a pool of olive oil and lemon juice. It is served with flat bread called *khobz* (pita), which is torn apart and used as a spoon to swipe it out of the bowl. Bites of fuul are followed by bites of onion, picked turnip, or radishes. The tea is served in small, clear glasses, not cups, sometimes with mint. Summer breakfasts are lighter. As is true of the Israeli breakfast, it is easy to see the Mediterranean roots of this menu: bread from the winter wheat; oil from the olive groves; and beans, lemons, and vegetables from the groves and gardens. For an Arab, there are few things more enjoyable than waking up to fuul, tea, and the sweet voice of Fayruz playing in the background. Fayruz is one of the most popular vocalists in the Arab World; her songs have transcended the decades since she first started performing as a child in the 1940s.

7

Jerusalem

Jerusalem celebrated its 3,000th anniversary in 1996. Even before it came under Hebrew rule, however, the city existed as a town called Jebus, one of the last to hold out against the Israelites. Located atop the Judean Hills, Jebus was not at a crossroads of trade, neither did it have a particularly defensible site. The major trade routes paralleled the coast to the west or ran along the plateau on the other side of the Jordan Rift Valley. The Judean Hills were just too rugged to invite much regular commercial transit. Furthermore, the hill on which Jerusalem was built, the original Mount Zion, was but one among many, and not even the highest.

The only site advantage Jerusalem had was a spring, today known as the Gihon. Fresh water, a precious resource in the dry world, gushed forth from the ground at the base of the hill. Gihon, in fact, means "to gush forth." The availability of water, combined with the relative location of Jebus, drew the attention of David, the Hebrew king. He needed a place for a new capital city, a place that was central to the newly unified nation of the Israelites. More specifically, he needed a location that was on the border between the northern and southern tribes (a location like Washington, D.C., which was chosen as the capital because it was on the boundary between the North and the South in the United States). Jebus met the requirements, so it was conquered and became Jerusalem.

When the Ark of the Covenant was brought to Jerusalem from Schechem (today's Nablus), the city became not only a political capital, but the Israelites' spiritual center as well. The Ark of the Covenant was the chest in which the Ten Commandments that were given to Moses were kept. On Mount Moriah, King David's son Solomon built a temple (the First Temple) to house the Ark. The temple also became the house in which Yahweh, the God of the Jews, was believed to reside. Today it is called the First Temple. Built in the tenth century B.C., it lasted for more than three centuries, only to be destroyed by the Babylonians when they conquered Judah. The captivity of the Jews in Babylon was short, however, and when they started returning to Jerusalem, they built the Second Temple on the same site. Eventually King Herod the Great rebuilt that temple, but it, too, was destroyed. Nothing remains of either temple, except a small ivory pomegranate, an ancient symbol of fertility, on display in the Israeli Museum.

What does remain is the platform built by King Herod to give the Temple Mount a broader top. One of the walls built to support the platform is what Jews today call the Western Wall. It is not the western wall of the temple; rather, it is the western wall of the mount on which the temple used to stand. The Western Wall reminds Jews of King Solomon's temple and the presence of God in the city of Jerusalem. Even Pope John Paul II, late head of the world's Roman Catholic community, prayed there when he visited Jerusalem in 2000.

As a result of the 1967 Arab-Israeli War, the Old City of Jerusalem, and with it the Temple Mount, came under Israeli

Jewish men pray at the Western Wall in Old City Jerusalem. Jews venerate the Western Wall, which dates to the first century B.C., because it is the only remnant of the sacred Temple of Jerusalem.

control. They cleared away a Moroccan Arab neighborhood in front of the Western Wall, and turned the space into a vast open plaza. The part closest to the Western Wall became an outdoor synagogue. Prayers go on there all the time, but Friday night is an especially busy time since Shabbot begins at sundown on Friday. Streaming into the Western Wall plaza every Friday night are processions of Hasidic Jews dressed as if they still lived in seventeenth-century Hungary, Lithuania, or Germany.

Today, the Western Wall is a popular place for Jewish boys to have their bar mitzvah, that is, their induction into manhood on their 13th birthday. Torah portions are read from the scrolls that are brought out into the open from a richly decorated ark, or chest. Men pray, women watch from the sidelines, and at the end of the ceremony friends and relatives throw candy. Space in front of the Western Wall is partitioned so that there is a men's side and a women's side. Bat mitzvahs, for young women, are held on their side of the partition. The purpose of approaching the wall is to pray, to draw as close to God as possible while still on Earth. Distractions—such as women in the men's prayer area, for instance—are minimized. Dress must be modest and the head must be covered. The Western Wall, as the only surviving reminder of the Temple on the landscape, makes Jerusalem the holiest city in the world for Jews.

Christians also revere Jerusalem as the holiest city in the world. In fact, there was a time in Christian history when they fought to gain possession of the city and its holy sites. That was a period known as the Crusades. However, Christian control of Jerusalem lasted less than a century. Nevertheless, a Christian presence remained. Today, various Christian churches own the holiest sites in and near Old Jerusalem that are connected with the life of Jesus, and with that they seem satisfied. In fact, some Christian groups attach more significance to these sites than others. The Roman Catholic and Greek Orthodox churches stress the value of a pilgrimage to the Holy Land. Protestant Christians do not, although many Protestants do visit the Holy Land and its sacred structures, sites, and landscapes.

What are the most important Christian sites in Jerusalem? The holiest church in the Christian world anchors the so-called Christian quarter of the Old City. It is called the Church of the Holy Sepulchre. The church was built over the sepulchre, or tomb, of Christ, the tomb from which he arose on the first Easter Sunday. It also encompasses the place of the

Crucifixion, known as Calvary or Golgotha. The original building on the site dates to the reign of the Roman Emperor Constantine. When he permitted the Christians of the Roman Empire to worship freely in the fourth century A.D., churches started marking all of the important Christian sites in the Holy Land. In fact, Constantine's mother, Queen Helena, was the first to visit Jerusalem and identify the most important places in Jesus' life. Constantine's basilica was rebuilt several times. The church there today is essentially a Crusader structure. It is shared by six Christian sects. The Greek Orthodox, Roman Catholic, and Armenian Apostolic churches have jurisdiction over most of the Church of the Holy Sepulchre. The Syrian Orthodox, Coptic (Egyptian), and Ethiopian churches also have small chapels. The Ethiopian monks have established a monastery on the roof. The church is open to all, however, and pilgrims come from around the world to draw closer to God at the site of his resurrection. Because the various churches do not always agree on how the church should be managed, however, a Muslim family has held the key to the front (and only) door for centuries.

In addition to the Church of the Holy Sepulchre, there are many other sites in the Old City that are connected with the last days of Jesus's life. The Roman Catholics have marked them on the landscape as the Stations of the Cross. Each station recounts a different event in "the Passion" of Jesus. Walking the Via Dolorosa ("way of sorrows") all the way to the tomb is an ongoing event in Jerusalem. Those Stations of the Cross are symbolized on the walls of virtually every Catholic church in the world. Every Catholic church is therefore tied to the events and landscapes of Jerusalem. Outside the city walls, the most important nearby sites are on the Mount of Olives. It was here that Jesus taught his disciples to pray the Lord's Prayer, wept over the fate of Jerusalem, and was betrayed by the kiss of Judas. The defining events of Christianity happened in Jerusalem.

The Church of the Holy Sepulchre in Old City Jerusalem is shared by six Christian sects—Greek Orthodox, Roman Catholic, Armenian Apostolic, Syrian Orthodox, Coptic (Egyptian), and Ethiopian. Christians revere the church, because it is believed to stand on the site where Jesus Christ was crucified and buried. The Ethiopian monastery is pictured here.

Jerusalem is also important to Muslims. It is the third-holiest city in the Islamic world, outranked only by Mecca and Medina. In fact, before Muslims prayed facing Mecca, they prayed facing Jerusalem. What happened here according to the Islamic scriptures? From Mount Moriah, the very place where the First Temple was located, Muhammad ascended to heaven to enter the presence of God. This is known as Muhammad's "night journey." In a single night, Muhammad left Mecca, rode a great steed called Boraq to Jerusalem, ascended to heaven (meeting Moses and Jesus on the way), talked with God, and returned again to Earth. The place where Muhammad ascended is now occupied by the Dome of the Rock, the first important Islamic structure ever built. It dates to A.D. 791, and its magnificence has transcended the centuries. It is not a mosque (although there is a prayer area in it), but a monument to a defining event in Islamic history. Nearby, however, there is the Al Aqsa Mosque, which means "the farthest mosque." Jews call the mount on which both the Dome of the Rock and the Al Aqsa Mosque are located the Temple Mount; Muslims call the mount on which both the Dome of the Rock and Al Aqsa Mosque are located the Haram Al-Sharif, which means the "noble sanctuary." Among the other buildings, there is a small mosque honoring Boraq. It is the place where Muhammad tied his horse before journeying off to the heavens.

Muslims, Jews, and Christians revere the same city, Jerusalem. It has been endowed with much holiness, but apparently not enough for everyone to have a share. Muslims fight with Jews over who should be in control. Jews fight with other Jews over who is allowed to go to the top of the Temple Mount. One Christian sect fights with another Christian sect over who has custody over the holy places. If ever a place needed "shared sovereignty" it is Jerusalem. The following list illustrates the incredible diversity of this magnificent, yet troubled, city.

Jerusalem: Seven Gates to Cultural Diversity

A city of many religions.
Judaism, Christianity, Islam

A city of many sabbaths.
Friday, Saturday, Sunday

A city of many calendars.
Gregorian, Jewish, Islamic

A city of many symbols.
Star of David, the Cross, the Crescent

A city of many languages.
Arabic, Hebrew, English, Armenian, Russian

A city of many alphabets.
Hebrew, Arabic, Roman, Armenian, Syriac, Greek,
Japanese

A city of many flags.
Israeli, Palestinian, UN, Vatican, Greek Orthodox

CHAPTER

8

Israel Looks Ahead

I srael is a small country, but it is one with a well-known history and a well-known record of current events. Within the territory controlled by the government in Jerusalem today are two distinct peoples, Israeli Jews and Palestinian Arabs. Their roots both go back to the earliest history of the region; their religions arose from the same patriarch, Abraham; their languages share a common ancestor; and their cultures have shaped proud identities. Yet, they see different futures and worry for their children. Israelis, and Jews around the world, worry about the very survival of the State of Israel, an independent country established for the Jews after World War II. Palestinians, and other Arabs around the world, worry that they will never have an independent country of their own. Both Israelis and Palestinians fear the worst: no country, no future. Yet, they both want the same land, the land between the eastern Mediterranean shoreline and the Jordan River.

Peace has come to two of Israel's frontiers. Treaties were signed with Egypt (1979) and with Jordan (1994), but not with Syria or Lebanon. In 2006, in fact, the Hezbollah militants, who control southern Lebanon, staged a cross-border raid into Israel. Hezbollah is an Islamic political party with an armed militia of its own. It is heavily backed by Iran and Syria. The Israeli Defense Forces responded to the raid (and the kidnapping of two Israeli soldiers) with a massive aerial bombing campaign, the deployment of troops into southern Lebanon, and a blockade of Lebanon's ports and airspace. Hezbollah rockets landed as far south as Hadera, 50 miles south of the border. Israeli bombing raids pummeled most of Lebanon, especially the area south of the Litani River. Damage to Lebanon's infrastructure was widespread and the civilian death toll was high, precipitating much international condemnation.

Within Israel and the Palestinian Territories, the Palestinians themselves are not at peace with the government that controls their future, the Israeli government in Jerusalem. Peace talks between Israeli authorities and the Palestinians began in the early 1990s, stalled in the latter part of the decade, and collapsed completely in the early twenty-first century. Major problems still have to be solved, and the country awaits the resumption of peace efforts. Among the most important issues are (1) the existence of Jewish settlements in the West Bank and East Jerusalem, (2) the status of the Palestinian refugees and their "right-of-return" to their homes and villages, and (3) the fate of Jerusalem, which both sides want for religious as well as political reasons.

By whatever name, Israel or Palestine, the land at the southern end of the western Fertile Crescent is probably the least desirable in the entire Fertile Crescent. Water is the source of fertility in the dry world, and there is just too little water for the country's 11 million people, especially when neighboring (and even drier) Jordan makes demands on some of the same water resources as Israel. Yet, water is practically the region's only natural resource, save for a few minerals and now natural gas. When that water is combined with human ingenuity, however,

A Palestinian woman and her child walk past an Israeli woman and her child in Jerusalem. Both Israelis and Palestinians have deep roots in the Holy Land and many are committed to creating a two-state system within the borders of Israel. However, long-standing animosities between the two groups may ultimately block the creation of an independent Palestinian state.

even deserts can be brought into economic production and turned over to livable cities. The Jordan Valley was brought to life with drip irrigation and Tel Aviv was built on the Jaffa Orange. Indeed, one of the lessons that Israel has taught the world is the power of human resources, in the form of both brains and brawn, to transform the landscape and build an economy. Today, there are millions of Israelis and millions of Palestinians in the country known on the map as Israel. Working together, they have more to gain than working separately. They can create a larger market, have a greater diversity of labor, and have a larger amount of brainpower to build a world-class economy.

Whether the Israelis and Palestinians will exist as one state or two remains an open question. To an outsider, the region seems like a perfect place for testing the power of multiculturalism. If two distinct cultures that are distrustful of each other can get along in Israel, multiculturalism might really be the future of the world. Yet, both the Israelis and the Palestinians have affirmed their commitment to a two-state solution, not a multicultural solution, to their ongoing animosity. Drawing a line between the two peoples, however, as settlement patterns now stand, seems almost impossible, particularly around Jerusalem. Moreover, the Israelis see a two-state solution differently from the Palestinians; they see the State of Israel as retaining ultimate authority over a state of Palestine. The Palestinians, on the other hand, see a two-state solution as giving birth to an independent state of Palestine and in no more than two pieces. And what would happen to Jerusalem? How would it be divided? Which of the two states would have authority to call Jerusalem its capital? These questions will have to be answered.

The people of the Holy Land look forward to a day when they need not fear for their lives, nor the future of their children. At different points in time, both Jews and Arabs have been in the crosshairs of history. Their religions are intimately attached to events that took place in Jerusalem, and their histories are intimately attached to places in the western Fertile Crescent. Because they both have such deep roots there, they both envision a long-term future there. Unfortunately, they envision a future separate from the other. Perhaps only the international community can make a difference in assuring the survival of Israel and the emergence of an independent Palestinian state. Or, perhaps a truly multicultural federation of peoples could become a model for other ethnically challenged areas of the world.

Facts at a Glance

Physical Geography

Location Middle East, bordering the Mediterranean Sea, between Egypt and Lebanon

Area Total: 8,020 square miles (20,770 square kilometers); land: 7,850 square miles (20,330 square kilometers); water: 170 square miles (440 square kilometers)

Climate and Ecosystem Temperate; hot and dry in southern and eastern desert areas

Terrain Negev Desert in the south; low coastal plain; central mountains; Jordan Rift Valley

Elevation Extremes Lowest point is the Dead Sea, -1,339 feet (-408 meters); highest point is Har Meron, 3,963 feet (1,208 meters)

Land Use Arable land, 15.45%; Permanent crops, 3.88%; Other, 80.67% (2005)

Irrigated Land 749 square miles (1,940 square kilometers) (2003)

Natural Hazards Sandstorms may occur during spring and summer; droughts; periodic earthquakes

Environmental Issues Limited arable land and natural freshwater resources pose serious constraints; desertification; air pollution from industrial and vehicle emissions; groundwater pollution from industrial and domestic waste, chemical fertilizers, and pesticides

People

Population 6,352,117 (includes approximately 187,000 Israeli settlers in the West Bank, approximately 20,000 in the Israeli-occupied Golan Heights, and fewer than 177,000 in East Jerusalem); males, 3,165,860; females, 3,186,257 (July 2006 est.)

Population Density 757 people per square mile (292 per square kilometer)

Population Growth Rate 1.18% (2006 est.)

Net Migration Rate 0 migrant(s)/1,000 population (2006 est.)

Fertility Rate 2.41 children born/woman (2006 est.)

Life Expectancy at Birth Total Population: 79.46 years; male, 77.33 years; female, 81.7 years (2006 est.)

Median Age 29.6 years; male, 28.8 years; female, 30.5 years (2006 est.)

Ethnic Groups	Jewish, 80.1% (Europe/America-born, 32.1%; Israel-born, 20.8%; Africa-born, 14.6%; Asia-born, 12.6%); non-Jewish, 19.9% (mostly Arab) (1996 est.)
Religions	Jewish, 76.5%; Muslim, 15.9%; Arab Christians, 1.7%; other Christian, 0.4%; Druze, 1.6%; unspecified, 3.9% (2003)
Literacy	(age 15 and over can read and write) Total population: 95.4%; male, 97.3%; female, 93.6% (2003 est.)

Economy

Currency	New Israeli shekel (ILS) (NIS is the currency abbreviation; ILS is the International Organization for Standardization (ISO) code for the NIS)
GDP Purchasing Power Parity (PPP)	$140.1 billion (2005 est.)
GDP Per Capita (PPP)	$22,300 (2005 est.)
Labor Force	2.42 million (2005 est.)
Unemployment	8.9% (2005 est.)
Labor Force by Occupation	Agriculture, forestry, and fishing, 2.6%; manufacturing, 20.2%; construction, 7.5%; commerce, 12.8%; transport, storage, and communications, 6.2%; finance and business, 13.1%; personal and other services, 6.4%; public services, 31.2% (1996)
Industries	High-technology projects (including aviation, communications, computer-aided design and manufactures, medical electronics, fiber optics), wood and paper products, potash and phosphates, food, beverages, and tobacco, caustic soda, cement, construction, metal products, chemical products, plastics, diamond cutting, textiles, footwear
Exports	$40.14 billion f.o.b. (2005 est.)
Imports	$43.19 billion f.o.b. (2005 est.)
Leading Trade Partners	*Exports*: U.S., 36.8%; Belgium, 7.5%; Hong Kong, 4.9% (2004) *Imports*: U.S., 15%; Belgium, 10.1%; Germany, 7.5%; Switzerland, 6.5%; UK, 6.1% (2004)
Export Commodities	Machinery and equipment, software, cut diamonds, agricultural products, chemicals, textiles and apparel
Import Commodities	Raw materials, military equipment, investment goods, rough diamonds, fuels, grain, consumer goods

Transportation	*Roadways*: 10,711 miles (17,237 kilometers)—including 78 miles (126 kilometers) of expressways (2002); *Airports:* 51–28 with paved runways (2005)

Government

Country Name	Conventional long form: State of Israel; conventional short form: Israel; local long form: Medinat Yisra'el; local short form: Yisra'el
Capital City	Jerusalem (Israel proclaimed Jerusalem as its capital in 1950, but the U.S., like nearly all other countries, maintains its Embassy in Tel Aviv)
Type of Government	Parliamentary democracy
Head of Government	Prime Minister Ehud Olmert (since May 2006)
Independence	May 14, 1948 (from League of Nations mandate under British administration)
Administrative Divisions	6 districts (mehozot, singular—mehoz); Central, Haifa, Jerusalem, Northern, Southern, Tel Aviv

Communications

TV Stations	17 (plus 36 low-power repeaters) (1995)
Phones	(including cellular): 10.2 million (2004)
Internet Users	3.2 million (2005)

* Source: *CIA-The World Factbook* (2006)

996 B.C.	Jebus conquered by King David, renamed Jerusalem and made capital.
920	First Temple built in Jerusalem by King Solomon.
586	First Temple destroyed by the Babylonians.
515	Second Temple built in Jerusalem.
A.D. 30	Jesus of Nazareth crucified at Golgotha outside Jerusalem's city walls.
66	Jewish Revolt against the Romans.
70	Jerusalem conquered and Second Temple destroyed by the Romans.
73	Last stronghold of the Zealots on Masada conquered by Roman legions.
335	Church of the Holy Sepulchre consecrated in Jerusalem.
636	Jerusalem conquered by the First Muslim Empire.
691	Muslim Dome of the Rock built in Jerusalem on what was probably the site of Solomon's Temple.
1099–1187	Christian Crusader states established in the "Holy Land."
1897	First World Zionist Congress in Basel, Switzerland.
1910	First kibbutz established near the Sea of Galilee.
1916–17	Arab Revolt against the Ottoman Empire.
1917	Balfour Declaration expresses British sympathy with "Jewish Zionist aspirations"; British troops led by General Allenby take Jerusalem from the Ottomans.
1920	Great Britain given Mandate of Palestine by the League of Nations.
1929	Riots at the Western Wall in Jerusalem between Palestinians and Zionists.
1939–45	Nazi Holocaust decimates Jewish population of Central and Eastern Europe.
1947	UN Partition Plan envisions separate Jewish and Arab states.
1948	Israel proclaims independence on May 14.
1948–49	First Arab–Israeli War.
1949	Israel is admitted to the United Nations.

1950	Jerusalem proclaimed official capital city of Israel.
1956	Suez War begins when Israel invades Egypt.
1964	Palestinian Liberation Organization (PLO) is formed.
1967	Six-Day War takes place June 5–10; Israel seizes West Bank, Gaza Strip, Sinai Peninsula, and the Golan Heights.
1969	Yasser Arafat becomes president of the PLO.
1972	Israeli athletes at Munich Olympics assassinated by Palestinian guerrillas.
1973	Yom Kippur War takes place October 6 to 24.
1974	Israel and Syria agree to the establishment of a UN Disengagement Observer Force (UNDOF) on the Golan Heights.
1977	Egyptian president Anwar Sadat visits Jerusalem at the invitation of Israeli prime minister Menachem Begin.
1979	Peace Treaty signed in Washington, D.C., between Israel and Egypt.
1980	Israel annexes "East Jerusalem," which includes the Old City.
1981	Israel annexes the Golan Heights.
1982	Israel completes evacuation of the Sinai Peninsula; Israel invades Lebanon.
1987–1993	First Intifadah (Palestinian Uprising).
1993	Declaration of Principles signed in Washington, D.C., between Israel and the PLO.
1994	Peace treaty signed between Israel and Jordan.
1995	Prime Minister Yitzhak Rabin assassinated by right-wing Jewish radical.
1996	Yasser Arafat elected president in first elections held by Palestinian Authority.
1999–2000	Talks between Israel and Syria take place in the United States.
2000	Ariel Sharon and 1,000 armed soldiers enter the Haram Al-Sharif (Temple Mount) in Jerusalem provoking the ire of Palestinians.
2000–2005	Second Intifadah (Palestinian Uprising).
2001	Ariel Sharon elected prime minister of Israel.
2002	Israel begins construction of security fence around West Bank.

2004 Yasser Arafat, PLO chairman, dies.

2005 Mahmoud Abbas elected president of Palestinian Authority; all Israeli settlers and soldiers withdraw from Gaza Strip.

2006 Prime Minister Ariel Sharon suffers massive stroke and is replaced by an acting prime minister, Ehud Olmert; elections to the Palestinian Legislative Council give a majority of seats to Hamas, a terrorist organization; Israel goes to war with Hezbollah militias in southern Lebanon.

Bibliography

Central Intelligence Agency. The World Factbook, 2006.
   http://www.odci.gov/cia/publications/factbook/geos/is.html

Efraim, Orni, and Elisha Efrat. *Geography of Israel.* Jerusalem: Israeli
   Program for Scientific Translations, 1964.

Held, Colbert. *Middle East Patterns,* 4th ed. Boulder, Colo.: Westview Press,
   2005.

"Special Report: The Future of Israel." *Newsweek.* April 1, 2002, pp. 22–50.

Armstrong, Karen. *Jerusalem: One City, Three Faiths.* New York: Alfred A. Knopf, 1996.

Benvenisti, Meron. *City of Stone: The Hidden History of Jerusalem.* Berkeley: University of California Press, 1996.

Cahill, Thomas. *The Gifts of the Jews.* New York: Doubleday, 1998.

Drummond, Dorothy. *Holy Land, Whose Land? Modern Dilemma, Ancient Roots,* 2nd rev. ed. Terre Haute, Ind.: Fairhurst Press, 2004.

Farsoun, Samih K., with Christine Zacharia. *Palestine and the Palestinians.* Boulder, Colo.: Westview Press, 1998.

Freidman, Thomas L. *From Beirut to Jerusalem.* New York: Alfred A. Knopf, 1990.

Gerner, Deborah J. *One Land, Two Peoples: The Conflict over Palestine.* Boulder, Colo.: Westview Press, 1991.

Held, Colbert C. *Middle East Patterns,* 4th ed. Boulder, Colo.: Westview Press, 2005.

Israeli, Raphael. *Green Crescent Over Nazareth: The Displacement of Christians by Muslims in the Holy Land.* London and Portland, Ore.: F. Cass, 2002.

Metz, Helen Chapin, ed. *Israel: A Country Study,* 3rd ed. Area Handbook Series. Washington, D.C.: Library of Congress, 1990.

Murphy-O'Connor, Jerome. *The Holy Land: An Oxford Archaeological Guide from Earliest Times to 1700.* Oxford and New York: Oxford University Press, 1998.

Osman, Colin. *Jerusalem: Caught in Time.* New York: New York University Press, 2000.

Smith, Charles D. *Palestine and the Arab-Israeli Conflict,* 5th ed. New York: St. Martin's Press, 2004.

Spector, Stephen. *Operation Solomon: The Daring Rescue of the Ethiopian Jews.* New York: Oxford University Press, 2005.

Stone, Robert. *Damascus Gate.* Boston: Houghton Mifflin, 1998.

Web sites

The Bahá'is
http://www.bahai.org

Understanding the Israeli-Palestinian Conflict
http://www.is-pal.net/

The Jewish Virtual Library
http://www.jewishvirtuallibrary.org/

A Country Study: Israel
http://lcweb2.loc.gov/frd/cs/iltoc.html

Virtual Tour of Jerusalem
http://www.md.huji.ac.il/vjt/

Online Encyclopedia of Palestine
http://www.palestinehistory.com/

Index

Index

About the Contributors

DONALD J. ZEIGLER, Ph.D., is professor of geography at Old Dominion University, where he teaches courses on political geography, world cities, and the Middle East. A former president of the National Council for Geographic Education, Zeigler has written several articles that have appeared in geographic journals. In 2006, he received the Virginia Outstanding Faculty Award from the state council for higher education. He has traveled extensively in Israel and neighboring states.

Series Editor **CHARLES F. GRITZNER** is distinguished professor of geography at South Dakota State University in Brookings. He is now in his fifth decade of college teaching, research, and writing. In addition to teaching, he enjoys writing, working with teachers, and sharing his love of geography with readers. As the series editor for Chelsea House's MODERN WORLD CULTURES AND MODERN WORLD NATIONS series, he has a wonderful opportunity to combine each of these hobbies. Gritzner has served as both president and executive director of the National Council for Geographic Education and has received the Council's highest honor, the George J. Miller Award for Distinguished Service to Geographic Education.